# How to Choose Your Next Employer

# How to Choose Your Next Employer

Roger E. Herman & Joyce L. Gioia

with Andrew T. Perry

Oakhill Press
Winchester, Virginia

© 2000 Roger E. Herman and Joyce L. Gioia
All rights reserved. Reproduction or translation of any part of this work beyond that permitted by Section 107 or 108 of the 1976 United States Copyright Act without the permission of the copyright owner is unlawful. Requests for permission or further information should be addressed to the Permissions Department, Oakhill Press.

This publication is designed to provide accurate and authoritative information in regard to the subject matter covered. It is sold with the understanding that the publisher is not engaged in rendering legal, accounting, or other professional service. If legal advice or other expert assistance is required, the services of a competent professional person should be sought. *From a Declaration of Principles jointly adopted by a committee of the American Bar Association and a committee of publishers.*

Without limiting the rights under copyright reserved above, no part of this publication may be reproduced, stored in or introduced into a retrieval system, or transmitted, in any form or by any means (electronic, mechanical, photocopying, recording, or otherwise) without the prior written permission of both the copyright owner and the above publisher of this book.

10   9   8   7   6   5   4   3   2   1

**Library of Congress Cataloging-in-Publication Data**

Herman, Roger E., 1943–
    How to Choose Your Next Employer / Roger E. Herman & Joyce Gioia;
  with Andrew T. Perry.
    p. cm.
    Includes index.
    ISBN 1-886939-37-3
    1. Job hunting. 2. Vocational guidance. I. Gioia, Joyce L. (Joyce Lea),
  1947–   II. Perry, Andrew T.
HF5382.7 .H465 2000
650.14—dc21                                                    00-039140

**Oakhill Press**
461 Layside Drive
Winchester, VA 22602
800-32-BOOKS
Printed in the United States of America

# Dedication

Each of us is privileged, at various times in our lives, to benefit from the advice and counsel of others who are wiser than we are. Sometimes we appreciate the guidance when we receive it; in other cases, we discover the treasure some years later.

Mentors, coaches, advisors, counselors, teachers, and other types of concerned caregivers contribute so much to our lives. Rarely do we invest enough time and energy to say "thank you."

Almost a decade ago, we served as faculty members for Coach University, a virtual learning organization helping people gain the knowledge and skills to become professional life-coaches. We both enjoyed the personal coaching we received from Thomas Leonard, the founder of Coach U. Thomas encouraged us, as we have encouraged our clients, to think about those special people who made a difference in our lives . . . then search them out and thank them. If they've already passed away, thank their loved ones.

As authors, we have a cherished opportunity to recognize special people in our book dedications. That's why this book is meaningfully dedicated to Lowell Grabow, Mike Ronca, Paul Gustafson, Frances Dyer, Annie May Tyler, and Joe Rashott.

Lowell Grabow, a career counselor at the University of Denver, had a significant influence on Joyce's life in her formative years. As she moved through college on an accelerated program, he was instrumental in her gaining the grounding and perspective on where her life might go.

Michael R. Ronca was the band director at Northwestern Senior High School in Hyattsville, Maryland, when Roger was a student there. Realizing that there was something more to this bass drummer who couldn't keep a beat, Mr. Ronca steered Roger into a management and leadership role that had a profound influence on the rest of his life.

Paul Gustafson, then head of the Sociology Department at Hiram College, opened new doors and encouraged a different style of thinking in Roger's life. He showed Roger how he could apply his knowledge experiences in different ways.

Frances Dyer was Joyce's science teacher in her secondary school years at Newman School in New Orleans, serving as almost a second mother. She taught from the book and from the heart, helping Joyce learn so much about the human side of life.

Annie May Tyler, from her humble station as a cook, taught Joyce the importance of love, tolerance, and overcoming life's circumstances to take charge of her own life.

Joe Rashott, the officer in charge of the 501$^{st}$ Military Intelligence Detachment at Fort Hood, Texas, was quite influential on Roger's life—both in his work as a Counterintelligence Special Agent and in his work as a Scoutmaster in the Boy Scouts of America. Life can have different balances with different perspectives.

Each of these things we learned from these valued advisors is significant in our lives today . . . and in your life. Think about these lessons and how they relate to the decisions you will make in the not-too-distant future as you consider choices about your career and about your life.

# Contents

Disclaimer .................................... ix
Introduction .................................. xi
Acknowledgments ............................ xiii

## Part One: Preparation
Chapter 1. What Are You Looking For? ............. 3
Chapter 2. How to Use This Book .................. 9
Chapter 3. Criteria for Selection: An Overview ....... 15

## Part Two: Making the Choice
Chapter 4. The Company ........................ 29
Chapter 5. The Culture ......................... 41
Chapter 6. Leadership and Working Styles .......... 57
Chapter 7. Working Environment .................. 71
Chapter 8. Benefits ............................ 89
Chapter 9. Compensation ...................... 109
Chapter 10. The Intangibles .................... 123

## Part Three: Conclusion
Chapter 11. Putting It All Together ............... 143
Appendix A. Scoresheets ....................... 151
Appendix B. Sabbaticals ....................... 183
Appendix C. Self-Employment ................... 187
Appendix D. Temporary Work and Temp-to-Hire ..... 191
Appendix E. On-Line Job Hunting ................ 195

Index ....................................... 201

About the Authors ............................ 219

# Disclaimer

This book is designed to stimulate your thinking. Although we've been fairly comprehensive in our approach, *How to Choose Your Next Employer* is not necessarily absolutely complete. We may have missed something that could be important to you as you make your next career decision.

We are not offering legal assistance or financial advice in these pages. We do raise some issues for you to consider, but for specific advice, we recommend you consult your professional advisors.

In today's world, people have more choices available to them than ever before in history. A great many of these choices revolve around lifestyle and workstyle. We can now design and drive our own careers, something practically unheard of not so long ago.

In our work as strategic business futurists concentrating on workforce and workplace trends, we have observed some significant shifts in the past few years. Under the influence of a variety of trends, the world of work will be substantially different in the years ahead.

While employers will continue striving to attract and select the ideal employees to meet their needs, applicants will have greater opportunities to participate in the mutual decisions. The abundance of positions available, relative to the number of qualified people available to fill them, assures that most workers will have plenty of choices of employment opportunities available to them.

You have the choices today. Our objective in this volume is to support your exploration and decision making. We'll give you things to think about . . . the rest is up to you.

Roger E. Herman and Joyce L. Gioia, Certified Management Consultants

# Introduction

Are you looking for a new job? Thinking about it? Unhappy in your current job? Do the columns upon columns of the same want ads, day after day, make you want to throw the newspaper out the window? Do you want something more from your next job? Something rewarding, something exciting, something better? Don't worry. You're not alone.

Looking for a new job just isn't the same as it used to be. In past generations—and even a few years ago—you sent out a batch of resumes and hoped for a few callbacks; you called a company on the recommendation of a friend; or, worse yet, you waited until someone called you. It's not that these methods are out of date or even irrelevant these days, but the situation has changed. The workplace has changed.

A booming economy and a technological explosion have combined to make unemployment drop rapidly over the past few years, and as we move through this new century, those conditions will only improve. The advantage is shifting. Employers—almost all employers—are constantly looking for new people. *The competitive advantage has shifted to you, the worker.* You are more in charge of your own career than any generation of workers in history. You are in the driver's seat. Now you get to make choices. You get to control your own career. You get to take back your life.

This book is designed to raise your antennae, so to speak, to these very changes and shifts in the marketplace. We will outline and discuss how the markets are changing, where the jobs are, and what you can expect both from a job search and from your new job. We'll discuss some of the new opportunities and benefits available to you in the workplace. We'll answer the easy questions, the tough questions, and some questions you may not even have thought about as you consider how to choose your next employer.

Think of this book as a tool—in fact, *the* tool—that can help you make the next crucial decision in your career. We've supplied a checklist at the end of most chapters in order to help you determine what you want. A section at the end will help you rank your desires and needs so that you have a clearer idea about what you want from your new job. We will help you avoid making a costly mistake—a mistake that could set back your career goals. You can also log onto our Website—*www.employerofchoice.net*—for more information about how to use your answers and for information about prospective employers.

The landscape is changing out there. You are more in command of your career than at any other point in history. You are able to make more of the choices that affect your life than ever before. This book will help you make those choices. This book will give you the information you need so that you can learn how to wisely choose your next employer. We'll stimulate your thinking to help you make choices that will be better for you. Your next offer is not necessarily the best move for you. Today, it's *your* choice, so make your choices carefully, intelligently, and knowledgeably.

# Acknowledgments

It's always a good practice to thank those who help you along the road of life, whether it is in writing a book, finding the right job, or strengthening our capacity to do what we want to do. Over the years, we have all thanked people who made a difference for us—schoolteachers, neighbors, employers, mentors, and so many others. We encourage you, dear reader, to do the same thing for those who have influenced your life.

Assembling a book like *How to Choose Your Next Employer* takes a lot of research and data management. We thank Jennifer Herman for the research help, April Pendleton for her creativity and gifted sense of design, and Cynthia Boren for helping us manage what could have become an overwhelming mountain of information.

A salute is in order for all the human resource professionals who gave us guidance and feedback to ensure our advice is realistic and suitable for the times.

Thanks to our colleagues in The Workforce Stability Institute who provided valuable insight into what works and what doesn't. We appreciate them sharing their experiences and perspectives. You can learn about these fine professionals at *www.employee.org*.

Our operations team at The Herman Group was, as usual, supportive beyond description. When busy consultants and speakers attempt to think, create, and write, having a highly competent team of people to manage business details makes a tremendous difference! A big salute to Kim, Cynthia, Carol, and April for choosing to be part of our team. Unwittingly, you all helped us write this book.

Our children were usually understanding when the call of writing pulled us away from family concerns. Thanks,

Samantha, Belinda, Jennifer, Melissa, Scott, and Maddie for your tolerance.

The professionals at Oakhill Press were astounding. Our head is bowed in awe and appreciation for the amazing work done by Paula Gould, editorial director. Ed Helvey has done a terrific job on the management end, and Craig Hines did a super job on the typesetting and design. Scott Herman's work on the book cover is sincerely appreciated.

Finally, a special acknowledgment goes to everyone who is searching for just the right employer. We have met so many of you over the past few years; hundreds have shared their stories, concerns, and fears when they talked with us after we spoke at a convention or management meeting where they were present.

## Part One
# Preparation

# 1

# What Are You Looking For?

Before we get into the specifics of how to choose your next employer and your next job, it's important to consider the kinds of things you'll be looking for in your next job as well as the sorts of career goals you have overall. As long as you have the skills and experience needed for whichever job you desire, your employment options are as varied as you want them to be. In some cases, companies are even willing to train you if you do not have enough experience. It's just a matter of figuring out where to start.

## Choosing a Career

*What kind of career are you looking for?* This question may seem obvious, but it's one that is sometimes overlooked by job seekers. Just because you're in a certain field now doesn't mean you want to stay there. Just because you have experience in a given area doesn't mean that's all you can do. After all, if you don't know what you're looking for, then you won't even know where to start.

Don't give up on *any* particular field or arena just because you don't have what you think is the "right" experience. Frequently, people who are hiring are looking for someone with a given set of skills, but not necessarily someone who has worked in any specific field prior to application. Think about your marketable skills before you send any letters or make any phone calls. Ask yourself what skills you may have that those making hiring decisions may need or desire, and then make sure to highlight those skills in your resume, cover letter, and initial conversations.

Don't be afraid to chase your "dream job." Read the want ads, the business section, and business magazines, and keep your eyes peeled for billboards, help wanted signs, and any other advertisements for jobs. Remember: you're in an advantageous position. Whether you're looking to move up in your current field or start all over, someone out there needs you. To get the ball rolling, all you have to do is apply.

## Marketing Yourself

*What are marketable skills?* Think for a moment about all your relevant abilities in the workplace. You may have skills from previous jobs or experiences that you didn't even know would be important later on.

### ASK YOURSELF: My Background

- ❏ Do I have clerical skills (typing, phones, research, organizational abilities)?
- ❏ Do I have any special computer proficiencies (software, network)?
- ❏ Do I have accounting skills (bill paying, books, office management)?
- ❏ Do I have physical skills that might be valuable (electrical, repair, maintenance)?

# WHAT ARE YOU LOOKING FOR? 5

- ❑ Do I have educational skills (teaching, teacher's assistant, corporate training, coaching)?
- ❑ What creative talents could I offer (graphic design, writing, decorating, artistic ability)?
- ❑ Do I have leadership and/or management experience?
- ❑ Do I have career-specific experience (driver, delivery, heavy machinery, quality control, manufacturing, food service)?
- ❑ Do I have people-specific experience (wait staff, retail, sales, human resources)?
- ❑ What in my educational background might be relevant (specific research, internships, past study, academic honors)?
- ❑ What in my personal background might be relevant (hobbies, travel, community service)?

Certainly this list of questions is only the beginning. Every individual will have his or her special set of proficiencies and abilities. Use this list to begin thinking about what sorts of skills and experiences you may have that will set you apart from the field and make you more marketable. What skills and expertise do you want to use, and what skills have little interest for you now?

## Job Expectations

*What do you want out of your next job?* Again, this sort of question may seem a little silly—until you really begin to consider the issue. Don't limit yourself to thinking about a few weeks, months, or even years down the road. Think about what you want your next job to offer you, immediately as well as down the road. Consider first what sort of field you will be looking into, and then build your expectations from there. In manufacturing, for instance, you may decide that you want to be a foreman within five years. If so, make sure there is opportunity for advancement. Conversely, if you're going into the management side of a larger firm, make sure there is room to grow laterally as well as vertically if you want the freedom to change the focus of your job within the same company.

Want to write? Interact with customers? Looking for freedom or responsibility? Decision-making power? Flextime? What have you liked most—or least—about past jobs? Again, make sure you're asking yourself *and* your potential employers the right questions.

## Opportunities for Growth

*Where do you want to be?* Don't shy away from asking specific questions about opportunities for growth. Look not only at the present opportunity, but also at what the organization will offer down the line. Have a plan in mind for where you'd like to be when you start, how soon you'd like to be promoted, and where you'd like to be in six months, twelve months, two years . . . as far into the future as you'd like to plan. Do you want to move up the corporate ladder or remain with the kind of work you do now?

## Length of Stay

*How long do you want to stay?* This is an important question in terms of planning for your future. In today's fast-paced and ever-changing marketplace, employees are not always looking for "permanent" positions. If you do want a long-term commitment from a company, make sure that ample opportunities for growth or advancement are available. If you're just looking for an entry-level position or an opportunity to gain experience, however, your criteria may change. Short-term concerns may be more focused on environment and learning, for instance, than on compensation or benefits.

Remember: you don't necessarily have to tell a prospective employer that you're not planning to stay a long time. In fact, you shouldn't—you may discover the right combination of benefits and advancement for you, and you may find career opportunities you didn't know were there when you started. Keep your options open. You'll probably find that your employer will want to keep options open for you, too—

# WHAT ARE YOU LOOKING FOR?

the company won't want to lose a valuable employee and will do what they can to keep you.

## Making the Choice

*So: What are you looking for?* You really should answer this question, at least in terms of career, before you go on. Do you want to be involved in health care or public relations? Catering or cable? Management or manufacturing? Retail or technical? We could probably offer a separate book for any given career path, but there are certain criteria for selection that hold true across the board. Once you decide what general field you'll be looking in, you can tailor the questions and options in this book to suit your specific needs.

The next chapter will explain how to use this book, and then we'll outline in general form some of the most common job choice criteria. The remainder of the book will be devoted to exploring your workplace options in detail. A final section will help you put it all together to get you ready to begin your search for your next job. Grab a pencil and get ready!

# 2

# How to Use This Book

Think of this book as a tool that will enable you to choose your next employer more easily and more efficiently . . . a tool that will help you make your choice a better one. This book will help you make the *right* choice.

We've designed the book to be just that—a tool. Now that you've finished reading the introduction and you have a good idea where we're heading, *and where you're heading*, turn to the back of the book to Appendix A. Have a quick look, and then come back to this chapter.

## Worksheets and Scoresheets

*There is a bit of "homework" ahead of you.* But it's not what you think it is. Appendix A is a series of statement lists and worksheets based on the content of the coming chapters—statements about what kind of company you're looking for, what sort of corporate culture you would like or need, what leadership and working styles you desire, what kind of a work environment is best suited to you, what benefits and compensation packages you want, and a few intangibles that can be crucial in your job search. Read through these lists before you read each chapter. Have the questions in mind as you go along. We have also provided space at the end of each chapter for you to write notes as you go.

In essence, this book is a workbook. It's an interactive experience. And, if you do the work—if you make notes as you go along and fill out the worksheets at the end—this book will *work for you*.

## A New Kind of Hardback Book

*This is not a coffee-table book.* Well, that's not entirely true, but it's a *different kind of coffee-table book*. It's the sort of book that we would rather you use as a coaster than as decoration. This is the kind of book that ought to have coffee rings and food stains on it. Why is that, you ask? If it has stains and dings in it, that means you're not afraid to *use* it.

We want you to:

- Highlight sentences and sections.
- Underline things.
- Fold down the corners.
- Jot notes in the margins.
- Spill your coffee on page 117 because you're so excited by what you're learning.
- Make lists in the spaces at the end of each chapter reserved for notes.
- Use the worksheets: Trust us. This is the good kind of homework. This is the kind of homework that will help you land *your dream job*.

# HOW TO USE THIS BOOK                                11

- Use your favorite pen or pencil to take notes. You use it for the other important things in your life—and this process will be an important experience.
- Have fun. Yes, you read right. Have a good time. As we just said, reading this book will be an important experience. It can also be fun, if you put in the effort.

## Making Things Easier

*We want you to be able to find the good parts quickly.* We think all the parts of this book are good parts, and we think you will, too. However, we've made some changes from the kind of business books and job-search books you're used to reading. Gone are the long, dull, marathon chapters of confusing advice and boring tone of voice. Instead, we've peppered this book with *things you can use in the real world*. Here are a few things you should keep an eye out for:

### REAL-WORLD PRACTICES

Real-World Practices sections will detail things that are going on out there in the real workplace, things you can expect to find every day in "dream" jobs. Real-World Practices will always appear in this font, and they'll always tell you about something that a great company out there is doing to make its employees happier and more satisfied with their jobs on a daily basis. Some of the things we've found out there will blow you away—ever heard of companies offering pet insurance? CEOs making bets with their employees? Building houses for Habitat for Humanity with your officemates? You will.

### HOT TIP

Looking for *the* one great idea that might make the difference between ending up in some lousy cubicle and finding a company where you'd like to spend the next few years of your life? The Hot Tip sections may just give you that little thing you need. They'll always look just like this, and they'll give you hints about ways to fine-tune your job hunt, new ways to read the want ads, ways to impress potential employers, and even ways to "test-drive" companies. There will be things you hadn't thought of. There will be things you didn't know you could do. There will be things in the Hot Tip sections to make you turn the corners down.

 ### YOUR JOB SEARCH

"All of this advice is great," you'll find yourself saying, "but what about me? I mean, how does pet insurance apply to *me*?" In the Your Job Search sections you'll find great advice for how to take what you're learning and apply all this great stuff specifically to your situation. We'll help you use what you know to your greatest advantage, and we'll help you design a job search just for you. In some sections of the book, we're talking to everyone. In the Your Job Search sections, it will feel like we're talking to you and only you. These sections will always look just like this, so you can find them quickly and easily.

### Reuse and Recycle

*Save this book!* In today's fast-paced and fast-moving working environment, it's likely you'll be using this book more than once. After all, you're almost never *finished* looking for a job. You're always on the lookout for your next opportunity, always learning skills in one job that you can apply to the

# HOW TO USE THIS BOOK        13

next. This attitude of learning doesn't mean you won't stay with your next employer for a long time—we hope you will, and you probably do, too. It's just that over time your needs and wants will change, and at that point you can use this book again, either to help you look for new jobs or positions within your current company or to help you look for an entirely new employment opportunity. (And in the interim, it can live on your coffee table!)

When you are finished with each chapter, use the corresponding scoresheet—make notes in the spaces we've provided. When you're finished with the book, use the scoresheets to rank your greatest needs (as well as to rank those things that are least important to you). You will give each statement a score ranging from -5 to +5, and then you can follow the instructions on the scoresheets and worksheets to help you more accurately and easily assess those criteria that will be most important to you as you set out on your job search.

## Once More with Feeling

Read each chapter more than once—once to get a good feel for the information, and a second time for scoring purposes. That way, you'll have a better idea what you're looking for, as you go through the scoresheets.

Remember: be as honest with yourself as you can. Read carefully and answer carefully. When you're finished, you'll be ready to flip open that newspaper, respond to that want ad, or click on that Website—*and you'll know exactly what you're looking for, and exactly what you want.*

Oh, and one more thing: you don't have to wash your hands before you pick up this book. There aren't huge color photographs and it's not printed on fancy paper. Save that for the oversized mail-order nature books that never get read. This book is a tool. Treat it that way. Read it. Use it. Reuse it. If you spill a little coffee along the way, we won't tell anybody.

Let's get started!

# 3

# Criteria for Selection: An Overview

The importance of any given benefit or selection criteria in a job search will of course change from person to person and from time to time. The trick is to figure out which items are most important to you and work from there. This chapter will outline some of the most important and most talked-about options in any job search, and the checklists within each small section will help you determine which chapters in part two of this book will be most important and most helpful to you.

## Type of Company

*What sort of company are you looking for?* Deciding what kind of company—not just in what field, but the makeup and styles of a specific company—you are looking for can be quite helpful as you begin your search. Deciding what industry to focus on is an important first step.

As the technology boom continues unabated, the concentration of jobs is moving into computer and technology-based fields, as well the service and health-care sectors. This is not to say that there aren't good jobs available in all fields, but if you are looking to maximize your potential value and aren't sure exactly what sort of career path you're most interested in following, it makes sense to follow the road to where the most jobs are. Something as simple as opening the want ads in your hometown paper can help you see where the highest concentration of jobs is for your consideration. But then again, you may not want to follow the more well-trodden path.

After you have thought about what industry you'd like to be in, consider what sort of company you'd like to work for within that industry. Think about these sorts of questions.

 **ASK YOURSELF: Type of Company**

- Do you want to work for a market leader or a start-up?
- Do you want to work for a company with solid name recognition?
- Do you want to work for a company with a high market share?
- Do you want to work in a large organization or a small one?
- Is it important to you to work for a company with a long history?
- Is stability—in market position and/or employee turnover—important to you?
- Do you want to know where the company has been, and where it's headed?
- Do you want a potential employer to be well known in the community?
- Is the quality of a company's goods and services a deciding factor?
- Is the inherent value—socially or otherwise—of a company's product a deciding factor?

# CRITERIA FOR SELECTION: AN OVERVIEW

Once you begin to narrow your search according to the kind of company you're looking for, the whole process will seem a lot less overwhelming.

## Company Culture

*What kind of company culture are you looking for?* Now that you know what kind of company you're looking for, you can begin to consider what you'd like that company to be like on the inside. We know this might sound a little "touchy-feely," but feeling good about the company you work for can be as important or even more important than any other factor in job satisfaction. There are as many different kinds of companies as there are job fields themselves, and the culture—or personality—of these companies varies widely from organization to organization.

You can learn a lot about a company from its literature. Ask for brochures about the company's products and services, and look for additional information on the company's Website. You can do research to find out even more information by looking for newspaper and magazine articles. You should also be prepared to ask questions in an interview, and you should look for opportunities to ask questions of the people who work where you would potentially be working. Finally, should you get the opportunity, simply look around at the workplace—what does it feel like? Here are some starter questions when considering the makeup of a company's culture.

 **ASK YOURSELF: Company Culture**

- How important to you are the standards to which the company holds its employees and its products?
- Are you looking for a corporate culture that values honesty and ethics?

- What sorts of honesty policies are important to you? Is the company open to honesty regarding past illnesses or addictions? Is sexual orientation an issue?
- Are you looking for a company that values experience and tenure?
- Does the company prize and implement new technologies? Is the availability of these new technologies important to you?
- How formal is the workplace? Are you looking for a "first-name-basis" company? Is dress code, formal or informal, important to you? Is it a "corner office" kind of firm, a cubicle forest, or an open office environment?
- Is it important to you that the company reward innovation? Support research and development? Be open to new ideas?
- How clear are internal communications? How would you rank the importance of clear and open communication between upper management and employees in the workplace?
- Is company spirit in evidence? Are things like corporate softball teams and logo coffee mugs, just to name examples, important symbols of company spirit to you?
- Look around. Are people having fun? Do they seem to enjoy their work?

## Leadership and Working Styles

*What style of leadership do you need to succeed?* The folks who work above you and with you can be immensely important in determining how happy you are at work. If you like and respect the people you work with, and if you respect and enjoy working for your boss, you are likely to be much more successful and much more satisfied with your job. Leadership needs and styles tend to vary with job requirements and with industry trends, but there are certain consistent qualities you can look for across the workplace. Here are some things to look for when evaluating your possible bosses and coworkers.

# CRITERIA FOR SELECTION: AN OVERVIEW

## ASK YOURSELF:
## Leadership and Working Styles

- ❏ What sort of boss are you looking for? Do you want a friend, a coach, or a taskmaster?
- ❏ Do you need to be pushed? Coached? Do you want to be on a first-name basis, or are you looking for a more formal and traditional relationship?
- ❏ How visible and accessible do you want your leaders to be? Are you more comfortable with your boss in an office, or out on the floor with employees? Do you need to be able to talk to your boss anytime about concerns you may have?
- ❏ How much responsibility are you looking for? Are the company leaders open to allowing you to take charge of problems and find your own solutions?
- ❏ How open is the company to change? If, for instance, you discover new, better, easier, or more efficient ways of doing things, will your ideas be considered or implemented?
- ❏ How does the company get work done? Will you have the opportunity to work on your own? In collaborative team environments?
- ❏ Will you have the opportunity, should you desire it, to seek promotions or transfers within the company? Does leadership limit or expand your future opportunities?
- ❏ How important is it to you to avoid "workplace politics"? Does it seem like politics are getting in the way at your potential employer? Are they working to get rid of workplace politics?

## Working Environment

*What kind of working environment are you seeking?* What do you want the actual workplace to be like in your new job? As the competitive selection shifts from employers to employees, more and more opportunity exists to seek out the sort of environment you've always wanted, even working environments you've never thought could be possible. Flexibility in office arrangement, job design, working hours, working conditions, facilities, and work/life balance is greater than ever before.

Don't be too quick to decide that a given factor in work environment might not be available to you or might not be out there at all. Look around and ask questions. The opportunities available to you might surprise you.

## ❓ ASK YOURSELF: Working Environment ❓

- ❏ Location, location, location. For some people, decisions about employment are based almost entirely on location. Where do you want to work? Downtown? In the suburbs? In a small town or in a big-city corporate campus? Do you need greenspace nearby?
- ❏ How important are commuting options in your decision? Is the office located near major highways? On public transportation routes? If not, does the employer offer transportation for those who don't own cars? Is it close enough/safe enough to bike to work? Walk to work? What are the housing options nearby?
- ❏ Must you actually be in the office to work for a given company? What are the telecommuting options? Virtual office options? Satellite locations?
- ❏ Is flextime an option and/or important to you?
- ❏ Do you want to work inside or outside? Do you want contact with customers? Do you want to be at a desk or out in the field? Do you want to work in production or in management?
- ❏ What does the workplace itself look like? How about the décor? Do you want to be a "Cubicle Creature"? Do you need an office? Do you want a wide-open workplace?
- ❏ How are working teams set up? Do people stay in one place or move around?
- ❏ Are there ample break areas? Eating opportunities? Is there enough parking? What other issues like parking matter to you? How about ATM and vending machines? Are there exercise facilities?
- ❏ Is there a commitment to workplace safety?
- ❏ What is the social environment like? Are families included in office parties and activities? Are friendships encouraged between employees? Is the social environment comfortable and friendly?

# CRITERIA FOR SELECTION: AN OVERVIEW

- Is the workplace relaxed or formal? How important are things like noise, color, and dress code to you?
- When you ask questions, and then compare answers to what you see in the office itself, does "what they say" match up with "what they do"?

## Benefit Options

*What benefits are important to you?* It can be very important to consider what kinds of benefits you want or need *before* you sit down to discuss a potential job or arrangement with your prospective employer. In fact, the kinds of benefits offered compared to the kinds of benefits you're seeking can be a valuable decision filter in narrowing and clarifying your job search. As with changes in the traditional workplace environment, changes in benefits have come as bargaining power has swung at least in part to prospective employees.

Types of benefits available range from the traditional health insurance and company cars to the more avant-garde types of benefits such as on-site pet care, concierge services, and clothing allotments. There is a certain tendency in today's marketplace away from traditional compensation packages and toward cafeteria plans and creative benefits offerings. A savvy job search can yield excellent benefits along with a good job.

### ❓ ASK YOURSELF: Benefit Options ❓

- What kinds of health insurance are you looking for? Do you need coverage beyond the traditional offerings? Are you looking for dental, maternal, vision, or other specialized care? Are additional coverages offered at discounts to employees? Can part-time employees piggyback on policies? What portions of premiums are employer-paid?
- What sorts of retirement or savings plans interest you? Are options

beyond the traditional 401(k) available? How much control will you have over the investments?
- What vacation packages are important to you? How long must you work before vacation benefits kick in? How much paid vacation is available? Would you be willing to take unpaid vacation if it is available? How much control do you have over your investments?
- Do you need on-site childcare? Elder care?
- Are you looking for other on-site services, such as tax, accounting, laundry, automotive, etc.?
- Will the company pay for field-related education? Are you seeking learning opportunities, either on-site or in local colleges or universities?
- Does the company encourage community service? Is it important to you that you be allowed to use some "company time" for volunteer activities?
- Are you looking for other experimental benefits, such as on-site pet care or pet-friendly workplaces?
- Do you consider flextime or commuting options benefits? What's available?

## Compensation Choices

*What kind of compensation package do you want?* While all the other categories and criteria are certainly important, money and compensation are certainly crucial as well. Today, though, compensation means more than just a paycheck. Compensation options and opportunities are as varied as the kinds of jobs out there. Ask yourself these questions when thinking about compensation.

**ASK YOURSELF:
Compensation Choices**

- How much money do I have to make when I start?
- How soon will it be reasonable for me to receive a raise?

# CRITERIA FOR SELECTION: AN OVERVIEW 23

- ❏ Does pay increase in kind with promotions and increased responsibility?
- ❏ How competitive is the salary range at this company when compared to the industry average? How competitive are the company's rates in the local community?
- ❏ What sorts of overtime payment options are available? How about compensatory time off?
- ❏ What kind of bonus packages does the company offer? Are there signing bonuses? Performance-based bonuses? Tenure-based bonuses? Can these bonuses be influenced by employee performance and achievement?
- ❏ Does the company offer profit-sharing opportunities?
- ❏ Are there compensation options available other than salary or hourly pay? Can you work as a contractor? On commission? Can you draw payment based on how well the company does? Are there equity options?
- ❏ Is the money worth the work?

## The Intangibles

*What sort of intangibles may make the difference in your choice?* All of the above aside, it's sometimes the small things that can make the difference. All the money and benefits in the world might not mean anything if that little voice in your head keeps nagging you, telling you that there's just something missing, that you're not happy. Here are some questions you might consider when deciding just what intangibles might be most important to you.

### ❓ ASK YOURSELF: The Intangibles ❓

- ❏ Is your current work meaningful? Would you be making a difference on a daily basis?
- ❏ Would you be able to see the results of your work at the end of the day, at the end of the week, or at the end of a project?

- ❏ Do you want responsibility and ownership of your own work? Is the work you do "yours"? Is accountability emphasized? Do you care about the job you do?
- ❏ Are there opportunities for you to become involved in community outreach through a potential job? Can you get involved in charity work? In case of tragedy or disaster in your community, will your potential employer do what it can to help?
- ❏ Is there something that we haven't thought of or listed that is important to you in your job search? Just because it isn't in print here doesn't mean it's not important. Add your own criteria as necessary.

## Moving Ahead

*What should you do with all these questions and answers?* Go back and look at these brief questions again. Each of the above sections is an overview of a larger chapter to come in Part II. Rank your individual answers in each section in order of importance, and rank each larger section in order of importance. You can then use this book like a handbook to help you determine the kinds of questions you should be asking of potential employers and, in a larger sense, what sorts of employers you should be seeking. You can use this book to learn more about the job selection criteria that are most important to you. We urge you to read every section carefully, however, even if it ranks lower in importance to you than another criterion. You may well run across ideas and opportunities you didn't even know were available to you.

We wish you luck in figuring out what you're looking for as you read on. Enjoy your current job search and those that inevitably will come in the future, as you continue to refine your criteria and make other choices.

# CRITERIA FOR SELECTION: AN OVERVIEW

## NOTES

Even though you're just getting started, we've provided some space here for you to make a few quick notes about your first impressions.

Which areas of your job search seem the most important to you right now?

_____
_____
_____
_____
_____

Which seem less crucial?

_____
_____
_____
_____
_____

Have you read about things you hadn't thought of before? Use the space here to jot down some initial ideas.

_____
_____
_____
_____
_____
_____
_____
_____
_____
_____

*When you've finished reading the book, compare your wants and needs with these notes. Then you can use these first observations to ensure you haven't left anything out as you begin your search.*

## Part Two
# Making the Choice

# 4

# The Company

Making choices about what industry you'd like to be in and what sort of company is right for you within that industry can be overwhelming at first. A quick glance through the newspaper or surfing across various job listing Websites will let you know that your choices are almost endless. Choosing a new industry or honing the focus of your current career is a crucial first step in any job search; after all, once you make even that first choice—what kind of job you're looking for—the entire process seems more manageable. Then, you can throw away some of the pages of your newspaper. You'll be able to enter keywords in Internet search engines. You'll have a better handle on what it is you want to do. You'll even be able to create your own job.

## Choosing an Industry

*What industry is right for you?* The answer to this question, and the reasons for that answer, are going to be different for every single person who reads this book. And it's not as easy a question as it sounds at first. The answer may *not* be something as simple as whatever industry you're already working in.

Do you like what your company does, but you're not happy with your job? You should then consider looking within your current field for other opportunities and for better opportunities. Are you tired of or bored with what you've been doing, or what your company has been doing? It may be time to consider a complete change to another field and/or another industry.

> **HOT TIP**
>
> Think about those times when you were a kid and it felt like the world was yours for the taking. What was your dream job when you were ten years old? Fifteen? What did you want to do when you were in high school or college? Are you doing those things now? If not, why not? What would it take for you to pursue your dream job? Did you always want to be a firefighter? An architect? A public defender? A carpenter? What is it, exactly, that's holding you back now? What do you have to do to remove the obstacles between you and what you really want to do?

## How to Make Your Choice

*How can you choose an industry, a new field, a new career path?* Choosing a new job, or at least deciding what you want to look for, is as simple as marrying the skills you already have to the skills required in any given field. You will be surprised how many of the skills and abilities you may have thought were career-specific will actually transfer to a new job in a new field. Just as companies sell themselves to their customers, you will be selling yourself to the companies. Make sure they know that you have the combination of ability and desire needed to work for them . . . and remember: in today's talent-short market, they're also selling themselves, as employers, to you. They need you to help them compete. Just as you can help them by being willing to learn a new skill set for a new job, they'll be ready to help you by teaching you and coaching you in order to help you fit in.

Don't shy away from a field or a job just because you don't think you have what it takes to work there. You'll never know until you try.

## Specific Choices

*What are you looking for in a specific company?* Once you've narrowed the field, it's time to start thinking about what you'll be looking for in an actual company. There are so many different kinds of companies out there, and so many different kinds of jobs within those companies, that you'll need to know exactly what you're looking for, as you begin contacting employers about potential opportunities. Knowing what you want from a company—and being satisfied with the company you choose—can go a long way toward finding happiness in your next job.

## Corporate Stability

*Are you looking for stability?* Most people are looking for stability in one form or another. Knowing that a company is financially stable usually helps employees gain confidence both in the employer and in the stability of their jobs—after all, most folks like to know that their jobs will be there for them next week and even next year.

Some people, however, are more interested in a risk/reward atmosphere, and may be looking for a start-up company or a struggling company. You might be looking for a situation where you could come in and make a difference right away, a situation where the issue of being stable is not as important as being able to take chances with the opportunity for larger rewards, both financially and in terms of your career. This type of decision may depend upon your personal financial situation and/or your position in your career; these choices will vary from person to person. You should invest some time considering what sort of risk/reward factor you're willing to pursue in your next job.

> **HOT TIP**
>
> Make sure that if you're willing to go out on a limb for a risky job or a risky company that you have something left to fall back on if things don't work out. You don't want to be left with a job that disappears when you have a stack of bills coming due.
>
> At the same time, it's important to make sure that you don't get stuck in a job that doesn't let you take enough risks or offer enough ideas for change. Find the right combination of stability and opportunity for where you are in your life and your career.

## Researching the Company

*What information do you need to know about a potential employer?* Ask a potential employer for any and all of the information they can provide to help make your decision easier. Get the company's history, its story, so that you know where the company has been and where it might be heading. Learning about a company's past successes and failures can help you discover things—like where it's been willing to take risks in the market, what it's done in times of prosperity, and how it survived in leaner times. Learning the story of a company can also make the entire process feel more personal and more human—it can help you look at the company as something more like a living organism and less like a corporate logo and a building.

# THE COMPANY

Many companies will offer literature in brochure, newsletter, or magazine form to prospective employees. Ask about higher-technology offerings, too, such as compact discs and Websites. Another good source of company history is in business publications and local newspapers. Do your research. The more you know, the better off you'll be.

## YOUR JOB SEARCH

- Go to the library. Look in search databases for articles and information about potential employers. Ask reference librarians for help.
- Ask around about any companies you're researching. Use your network of "folks in the know."
- If the company makes products, go to stores and look at what it makes. Look at the packaging. Look at the product itself. If it is a service-based company, ask around about how good it is at what it does. Look at who the company has as clients.

## Market Position

*Where do you want the company to be?* Do you want to work for a market leader or a start-up? Is it important to you to work for a company with solid name recognition? Consider what you want your business card to look like, or where you want to be in the production line or hierarchy, and what you want to be making.

There are certainly benefits in working for a market leader. Stability, salary, fringe benefits, corporate respect . . . all of these may be more accessible in a company with a larger market share, longer history, or with a greater name recognition in the industry. If these things are important to you, then look for how the company is perceived within its industry and within the business community as a whole. Do its employees speak at conferences? Are its leaders highly visible within the corporate community? Are the company's products and services widely available? Does it advertise? Do your peers know what the company is and what it does? Are feelings about the organization positive?

> ### REAL-WORLD PRACTICES
> Southwest Airlines reinforces its reputation through numerous speeches delivered throughout the country by its vice president of people and its vice president of people development, among others. As they share what they've accomplished and some of the methods they've used, they enhance the reputation and mystique of the company. Since they're out with other people in their field or related fields, they are accessible to receive inquiries about employment. And, by their titles alone, both their internal and external customers can see the dedication the airline has to its people.
> 
> One more thing: their advertisements are everywhere these days! Their slogan is recognized and their branding is widespread as a low-cost, high-quality airline. They are certainly seen not only within the airline industry but also across the corporate spectrum as a leader.

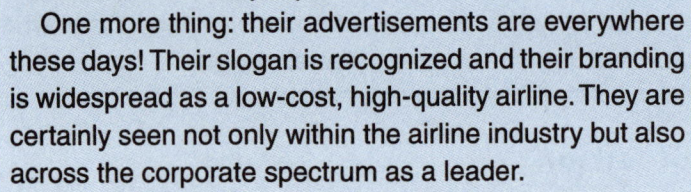

## Community Reputation

Do you want a potential employer to be well known in the community? More than just being recognized in a given field, some people find a high level of recognition within various communities an important factor in their job search decision. Look around the various communities where you live. Can you see evidence of corporate participation not just where you work, but where you shop or where you play?

# THE COMPANY

## REAL-WORLD PRACTICES

Kroger, a large supermarket chain, collects receipts from its sales in boxes at the front of their stores for local public and private schools. When a given school surpasses a certain dollar amount in Kroger receipts, the company donates classroom materials like computers and televisions to that school. In this way the community holds the company in high regard; the company is "giving something back."

## YOUR JOB SEARCH

- Look for corporate participation in local and national events such as charity fundraisers, benefit dinners, fun runs, and more.
- If community participation is important to you, ask potential employers for documentation of the ways they give back to the communities in which they do business. Are employees involved or is support limited to corporate financial donations?

Sometimes it's not just what a company does in the community that's important, but what sorts of opportunities are available to employees in terms of community participation. You can also ask what volunteer opportunities or programs are available to employees in whatever companies you may be considering. Can you use company time and/or resources to support causes that are important to you?

> **REAL-WORLD PRACTICES**
>
> The employees of Bank of America participate in Team Bank of America's Volunteer Network, a program that's sponsored by the company. Through this program, employees have opportunities to engage in a variety of volunteer activities that make a difference. Some of the worthwhile pursuits include restoring homes for senior citizens, fund-raising for charities, helping at homeless shelters, and cleaning up the environment. Team leaders learn skills like conflict resolution, speaking, and networking. Because they're working side by side with senior managers from other divisions, when they take the initiative, they garner attention. Some team leaders have been promoted at the bank as a result of their demonstration of leadership abilities in the volunteer setting.[1]

## The Importance of Quality

*Is the quality of a company's goods and services a deciding factor?* Scandals over poor quality or shoddy services in corporate practices make the news every day, but we rarely hear about overly high quality or outstanding service. The quality of the widgets a potential employer makes or the value of the service it provides can be more than a deciding factor in a job search—it can mean the difference between feeling happy in your job and in your life as a whole or not. After all, if you feel good about what you're doing—if you feel you're making a difference—you will obviously be happier in your job.

If the inherent social value of what any given company does is important to you, make sure you fully research not only that company's products and services, but that company's past history as well.

# THE COMPANY

> **HOT TIP**
> Check with organizations like the Better Business Bureau and the Chamber of Commerce in your town to find out about a company's reputation and past practices.

## SUMMARY

We think that in your job search, you'll find it's never as simple as just choosing what industry you want or what kind of company you'd like to work for. There are so many companies out there doing so many different things so many different ways. It's vitally important for you to really think about what you want out of a company before you begin your job search. Consider everything that will be important to you personally and professionally before you begin, and make sure you have those needs and wants really refined—before you make your choice.

## ASK YOURSELF: Choosing a Company

- What industry is right for me?
- What kinds of skills can I transfer from my current job to my next one?
- What do I really want to be doing? What do I want to be doing in one year? Five years?
- What have I always wanted to do? What's keeping me from that?
- Is there such a thing as an unrealistic career goal?
- How do I go about choosing a new field or a new career path? What is most important to me in looking for a new job?

- What am I looking for in a specific company?
- What am I looking for in a specific job within that company?
- How important is stability? Do I want a firmly established organization or a start-up?
- Is taking risks the best thing to do at this point in my career? Do I need more excitement than would be available in an older, larger, more stable firm?
- What information do I need about a company before I can make my choice?
- Where has the company been in the past six months? Ten years? Where is it headed in the future? Do they have a plan for the company? For me?
- Do I want to work for an industry leader?
- A community leader?
- How important is the quality of a company's goods or services to me?
- How important is the inherent value of those goods and services to me?
- When I think about working for that company, does it feel right? If so, why? If not, what's missing? Where can I find what I want and need?

1. Nancy Wong, "Volunteer Program Is a Springboard for Career Advancement," *Workforce* (July 1999): 18.

# THE COMPANY

## NOTES

Were there any questions in the company checklist that stood out to you? Were there any sections in the company chapter that struck you as particularly important or especially relevant to your search? Was there something you feel you should jot down now for later reference? Use this space to record your impressions, your ideas, your wants, and your needs in regard to the sort of company you'll be looking for.

# 5

# The Culture

Once you know what kind of company you're looking for, you can begin to fine-tune your search and look at more specific aspects of what you want in your new job. What do you want your new company to *feel* like? To *be* like? What will you need in a new job to feel at home?

Organizational structure, belief systems, the way things are done, the way people treat one another, and the way people within the organization treat external customers are all factors in the makeup of a company's culture. As you read through this chapter, consider which corporate cultural aspects are most important to you. Think about what you liked and what you didn't like about the places you've worked in the past. Keep in mind what sorts of cultural factors made you feel most comfortable and which caused you the greatest concern. Thinking about what you need from your next company—in terms of the way you want to feel about working there, about the people you work with, about the job you'll be doing—will help you in determining which cultural factors will be most important to you in your search.

## Styles of Working

*What if there isn't any one specific way you want to work?* Every corporate culture will be unique, just as every one of us is unique. It seems almost impossible that you will find *the perfect fit* in any single organization. However, you will want to look for the type of organization into which you will fit most easily. It will also be valuable to find the type of organization that will allow you to carve out your own personal niche. No one wants to be a robot, doing the same tasks the same ways, as everyone else. Search for a company that will allow you to be you, but one that will make it the easiest to be you as well.

### HOT TIP
Look around when you're at a job interview, or even when you're just out in everyday life. What sort of corporate cultures appeal to you? Where would you feel most comfortable? What kinds of people are you looking for in your next job? What sort of environment?

## Standards and Values

*How important to you are the standards and values of the company?* If high standards—in products, services, ethics, or otherwise—are an important part of your decision-making process, then look for direct and outward evidence of the standards of a given company. Most companies, whether intentionally or not, communicate the level of their values and standards in almost everything they do. Make sure that in the literature, as well as in the products and services of a given organization, there is plain evidence that the corporation is committed to "doing the right thing." Look at the quality of

# THE CULTURE

their products *and* of their people. Would you trust the services of a potential employer? Would you trust the people?

## Ethics and Honesty

*Are you seeking a corporate culture that prizes ethical behavior and honesty?* Be sure that any company you are considering displays both inward and outward signs of ethical behavior. If a company holds these values dear, it is likely that they will have a reputation for doing so in the business community. Ask around.

## Equality

*Are issues of equality important to you?* Do not shy away from asking employers about policies concerning race, age, sex, or sexuality. Most will be quite forthcoming, and you may be pleasantly surprised to discover that most good corporate citizens are actively working to open their doors to people from diverse backgrounds.

Again, your eyes may be your best selection tool here: do you see a variety of people working in the office? Are there any obvious discrepancies between management and frontline workers? Would you feel comfortable working there or not?

People of different backgrounds bring different perspectives to any given problem. Greater diversity generates better problem solving and decision-making, and makes the workplace a better place to be.

---

**REAL-WORLD PRACTICES**

A study conducted by The Hudson Institute and Walker Information—published in December 1999—reveals that the higher employees rate their employers on ethical standards, the more loyalty they feel. Of the 2,300 people surveyed, 55 percent felt positively about standards and

*continued*

loyalty. Unfortunately, only 47 percent believe that their leaders are people of high integrity.

If you're looking to stay with your next employer a long time, make sure that you consider not only whom you'll be working with, but also whom you'll be working for. Read the results of that survey again. They're pretty telling.

### REAL-WORLD PRACTICES

Joyce was engaged by Bellcore in Piscataway, New Jersey, to speak at the graduation ceremony for the 27 people completing the company's two-year Personal Development Program (PDP) for rising stars. She was struck by the age and cultural diversity of the group. Graduates were old and young, Black, Hispanic, Asian, and Caucasian. It seemed as if every conceivable combination of age and culture was represented.

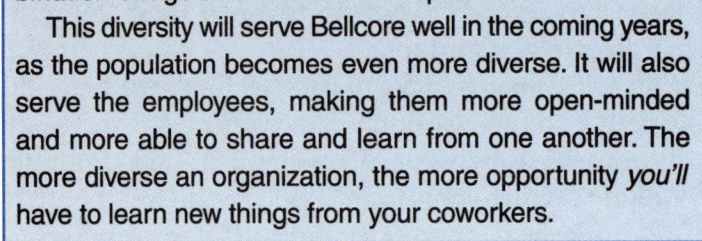

This diversity will serve Bellcore well in the coming years, as the population becomes even more diverse. It will also serve the employees, making them more open-minded and more able to share and learn from one another. The more diverse an organization, the more opportunity *you'll* have to learn new things from your coworkers.

## Valuing Experience

*Are you looking for a company that values experience?* If you're looking to stay with your next company for a long time, issues of experience and tenure will be important to you. A responsible employer doesn't try to push people into retirement just because they're 55, 65, or even 75. No matter what tasks these workers perform—from frontline work to top-level management—they are important and should be valued for their knowledge and experience. Be wary of joining a company that boasts of early retirees.

# THE CULTURE 45

> **HOT TIP**
>
> Contact local chapters of watchdog organizations that monitor discrimination in the workplace. They may well have lists of "best" and "worst" employers in your area and may be able to provide you with additional information about diversity in the workplace.

## Quality of People

*What do you need to know about the caliber of people who work for a company?* You want to work for a company that only hires the best people. Anyone who has ever worked with or for people who simply didn't make the grade knows how frustrating it can be to be held back by incompetence. Ask about the kind of work being done in the company; questions about problem solving and innovation can help you get at the sort of information you'll be looking for.

Find out how new employees are recruited. Does the company encourage employees to recruit their friends and acquaintances? People already working there will naturally want to recruit people they not only like, but also people they respect as well.

Consider how you found out about the position. The way companies recruit can signify the way they operate.

## Having Fun

*Do you want to enjoy your job?* A crazy question, right? Maybe not . . . think about how many jobs you've had, and how many you've actually enjoyed. People want to work hard, but they want to have a good time, too.

There are all sorts of ways to make a workplace fun; you should seek out employers who do so. If people enjoy their work and their coworkers, the environment is likely to be far more positive and, in the end, productive.

Organizations can engender a positive and lighthearted environment through such items and activities as office parties, event celebrations, team-building activities, social events outside of the office, company sports teams, and countless other means. Ask employers about what goes on in their office besides just work.

### REAL-WORLD PRACTICES

When Andrew was being interviewed for a job with Schwartz Communications in Boston, he was asked if he could "field." It seems the company's softball team was in need of a left fielder. We suspect that his positive response to the question was instrumental in helping him get the job.

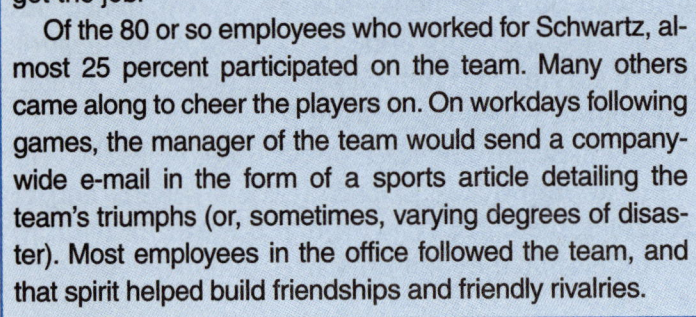

Of the 80 or so employees who worked for Schwartz, almost 25 percent participated on the team. Many others came along to cheer the players on. On workdays following games, the manager of the team would send a company-wide e-mail in the form of a sports article detailing the team's triumphs (or, sometimes, varying degrees of disaster). Most employees in the office followed the team, and that spirit helped build friendships and friendly rivalries.

### YOUR JOB SEARCH

● Think about the things that have made your jobs fun in the past, and think about the things that have made you miserable. It's sort of like the old joke about the guy who complains to his physician, "But, Doc, it hurts when I do this." The doctor replies, "Then don't do that." Don't join a company that makes you feel uncomfortable in the ways that your old company did. If you want company softball, then look for an organization with a team. If they don't al-

# THE CULTURE

ready have one, ask about organizing one. Go into your search knowing what kinds of "nonwork" things you'll be looking for in your next job, and then seek them out.

## Workplace Formality

*How formal do you want your next workplace to be?* Again, this question might be one that sounds a bit foolish on the surface, but it can be vital. What are you looking for in the actual work environment? Do you want to wear suits and dresses to work every day? Would you like to be able to call your boss by his or her first name?

The level of formality varies between companies and even between days, so make sure that you find a company that is a good aesthetic fit for you. If you're not comfortable going to work every day in jeans, for instance, then don't join a firm that dresses in a way you consider "way down."

> **HOT TIP**
> How friendly do the people in the company you're looking at seem to be with one another? Is there a feeling of camaraderie? Do people from various departments ever see each other? Consider what you'd like out of your next job socially as well.

## Technology Updates

*Is it important for you to work with the latest technologies?* If it is important to you to stay on the cutting edge in your work, then that may not only influence your choice of industry but your choice of companies within that industry. Certainly in any field there are companies that are always one step ahead of the times, and those that are always struggling to catch up. If you want to work with the latest developments in technology and equipment in any field, make sure to research what those developments are and which companies are using them.

### YOUR JOB SEARCH

- Know about and understand the latest and best technologies in your chosen field. Be able to discuss those you understand and demonstrate proficiency for those you know.
- Acquire experience in as many computer programs as possible.
- Look for companies that aren't afraid to try new technologies and advancements.

### REAL-WORLD PRACTICES

MGM Transport Corporation, High Point, North Carolina, a regional carrier of furniture from manufacturer to retailer, uses live audioconferencing to include people from North Carolina, New Jersey, and California in all staff, management, and sales meetings. Videoconferencing is used by TDS Telecom, Madison, Wisconsin, to include employees in remote locations in the company's ongoing training and development program.

## Rewarding Genius

*Do you want to work for a company that rewards ingenuity?* Most workers are looking for a job where their ideas will be not only heard, but also tried. New ideas are fun, challenging, and stimulating. New ideas move organizations forward. After all, it is most often the employees themselves who know how to improve upon existing practices or can best suggest new ideas or protocols. Be on the lookout for companies that are most open to change and innovation.

Don't think that this idea of ingenuity is limited just to research and development departments. There are smart and clever people at every level of every organization. Look for a company that is ready to hear ideas from *anyone* at *any* level.

A good indicator of whether a company you're considering prizes innovation is if they have a rewards system in place for top-drawer ideas and improvements. They might have plaques on the wall, revolving employee awards, mention of innovations in company literature. . . . If you can't find evidence of a company rewarding and even soliciting innovation fairly easily, you may be looking at a company that isn't listening closely to employees.

## Talking to Each Other

*How important to you are internal communications?* Have you ever been in a company where no one knew what anyone else was doing? Environments like that can be alienating, lonely, fractious, and frustrating. A company with good internal communications is inherently a better company. Think about it: A company with a solid communications structure and open pipelines is a company in which everyone feels like part of a team, in which the successes of one department are enjoyed and celebrated by all other departments.

Remember this: Most companies probably think they have good internal communications. Bosses and higher-ups may not be the right people to ask. If you have the chance to talk to people who work where you would be working, ask them a few questions, too.

Look for things like employee mailboxes, e-mail and larger information networks, and employee phone lists hung on office walls or cubicle partitions. Search out indicators of solid and effective communication like bulletin boards, newsletters, and posters.

## HOT TIP

Ask a prospective employer for a copy of the latest employee newsletter, a copy of a weekly memo, or, perhaps, to be added to the companywide e-mail list for a day or two. Being privy to these types of communications will really help you get a feel for how business is done there.

## HOT TIP

Look for evidence of strong *internal marketing* in any company you are considering. Remember that a corporation's employees are its customers as well, in that they need to be satisfied to stay, just as its external customers must be satisfied to continue to make purchases. Examples of internal marketing include newsletters and magazines; traditional advertising media such as posters or banners; strong evidence of person-to-person contact and interdepartmental contact; employee surveys; employee focus groups; interest and attitude surveys; audiotapes and videotapes detailing company projects, goals, or successes; product examples within the walls of the company itself; closed-circuit TV; intranet and Internet capabilities; special sales or achievement promotions; and general publicity about what the company is doing.

# THE CULTURE

> ### REAL-WORLD PRACTICES
>
> Until 1997, American Freightways Corporation, a large trucking company in Harrison, Arkansas, provided employees with a suggestion box and received a whopping one or two comments a month. Management figured the response rate had more to do with the feedback method it used than employees being so satisfied that they had nothing to complain about.
>
> To make offering comments and complaints more in line with current technology, and to bolster feedback, American Freightways began using a product called In-Touch, a confidential toll-free telephone number employees could call with ideas for improvements, reports of problems with managers and colleagues, and anything else on their minds.[1]
>
> The results of the new system were dramatic, as 150 to 350 employees a month began calling to comment. The company still trains employees to first contact managers with suggestions and concerns, but management realizes that some employees don't feel like they can talk about some things with their bosses. This medium is another way for employees to make their feelings known, and for them to know that someone's listening.

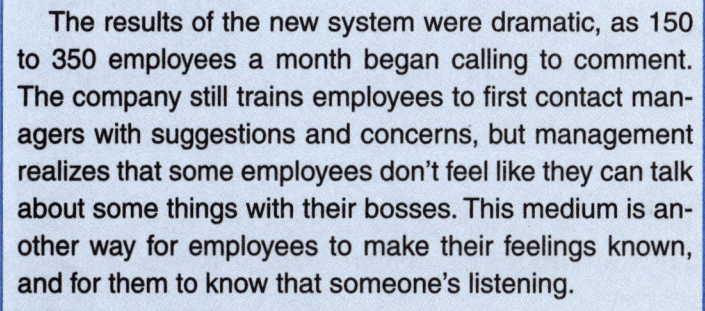

## Corporate Spirit

*How highly do you value company spirit?* There's a reason everyone on a baseball team wears the same uniform. Sure, it's so they can identify one another, and so that fans can identify them, but it's also so that they can really feel like they're part of a team. While you don't necessarily have to wear a uniform to work, that desire to feel like a part of something still applies.

From something as simple as logo coffee mugs and polo shirts to something as significant as, say, the pink Mary Kay Cadillacs, most companies—most companies serious about holding onto their employees, that is—provide some way for employees to identify with one another. We've already discussed team sports here, but rewards programs, apparel, company picnics, and the like can go a long way towards making you feel at home, a part of something.

### YOUR JOB SEARCH

- If you're looking for company spirit or company perks, do a little investigating to see what's available. Many stores and manufacturers sell their merchandise to employees at deep discounts. Want coffee? Work for Starbucks. Want to feel like a part of a community? Work for a bookstore that sponsors employee-reading clubs.

### REAL-WORLD PRACTICES

Modern International Graphics, Eastlake, Ohio, has a "nice catch" award for employees who spot a problem with a customer's printing job. When someone catches a mistake and calls it to the attention of a supervisor, the ritual begins. First, over the public address system comes the honk of a bicycle horn. Then company executives and salespeople parade through the printing plant with balloons and kazoos until they reach the workstation of the award recipient. The employee is presented with the prize: Ohio Lottery tickets. The tickets could be big winners—or not—but it's fun getting the recognition and a chance at some big money.

# THE CULTURE

> **REAL-WORLD PRACTICES**
>
> Manco, Inc., a manufacturer of "Duck Tape" and other products, has a culture that encourages fun as well as serious attention to business. A company ritual that endured for years captured Manco's pride, spirit, and personality: Duck Challenge Day. Each year, the company sets aside one special day to celebrate teamwork, creativity, and successes with special friends and colleagues.
>
> CEO Jack Kahl initiated Duck Challenge Day in 1990 with a simple bet. "If we reach $60 million in sales, I'll jump in the duck pond out front." They met their goal, and Jack plunged into the icy water as the Manco partners cheered him on. From then on, a new challenge was issued each year. By 1995, 59 partners had joined Jack for a celebratory swim in the bitter cold of winter in Cleveland, Ohio.
>
> Manco moved to its new headquarters in 1996, and the new pond was too small to continue the tradition. But Jack had a new challenge. If Manco reached $175 million, he would shave his head. Once again, the company surpassed the profit goal. Jack's haircut made headlines in business publications across the country, and even captured the attention of the *National Enquirer*.

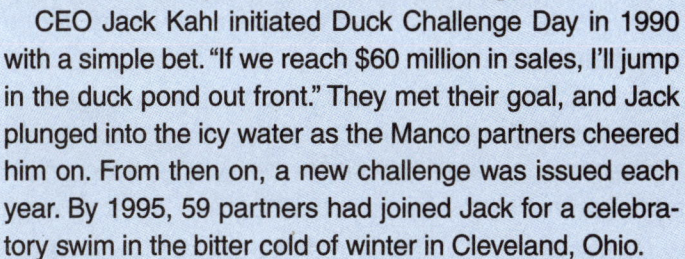

## SUMMARY

We're not saying you have to go right out and look for a company where the president shaves his head once a year, though we wouldn't discourage you. We simply want to point out that an organization's culture can be a huge determinant of how happy people are to be working there. Make certain that you have considered what you want and what you're looking for, *before* you sit down to talk to a company. Do your homework. Most of the answers to your questions should be easily available. And remember—if they aren't, you need to ask why.

## ❓ ASK YOURSELF: Choosing a Culture ❓

- What is it that I want out of the things that are tougher to define about companies? What kind of corporate culture appeals to me?
- In which ways do I like to work?
- How important are standards to me? Where and how do I rank quality of service? Of products? Of coworkers?
- How would I define *honesty* and *ethics*? How do I want my employer to define these terms?
- Where do I want honesty and ethics to rank in a list of items important to my employer?
- How important are issues of equality to me? Why are they important? Is there something about me that requires an employer to be more progressive? Do I need my employer to provide special services for me? Does this potential employer seem to be interested in racial, sexual, and age-based equality?
- Am I looking for a company that values experience? Am I an older employee who feels that the company may be looking for younger blood? Am I a younger employee in search of an older mentor? If I am thinking about staying in this company a long time, does it seem that this company will continue to want me?
- What kinds of people do I like to work with?
- How will this company help me enjoy my job more? How can I help the company?
- How can I have fun at work?
- How formal do I want the workplace to be? Do I want to be on a first-name basis with my bosses? What about dress code? Office layouts?
- What do I want an employer to do for me in terms of exposing me to the latest technologies? How can I get there?
- What am I looking for in terms of my employer rewarding new ideas?
- How important is it to me that everyone feel connected? How good are the communications in the company I'm considering?

# THE CULTURE

- ❏ Do I need for people to listen to me when I have ideas?
- ❏ How important is company spirit to me? Am I the company basketball-team type? Jogging club? Weekly dinners with my friends from work?

1. InTouch is manufactured by Management Communications Systems, Inc. An alternative system is offered by The Network, an Atlanta-based company whose toll-free lines are staffed with live operators. On duty 24 hours a day, they interact with employees by asking specific questions to clarify various points. The Network designed its own software program, prompting operators to ask the questions to achieve as detailed a report as possible from employees.

## NOTES

Were there any questions in the culture checklist that stood out to you? Were there any sections in the culture chapter that struck you as particularly important or especially relevant to your search? Was there something you feel you should jot down now for later reference? Use this space to record your impressions, your ideas, your wants, and your needs in regard to the sort of culture you'll be looking for.

# 6

# Leadership and Working Styles

Though the way business is done and the way leaders interact with employees could be considered a part of workplace culture, we believe these issues are important enough to warrant their own chapter. We can't even count the number of times we've heard someone note that their reason for leaving their last job was "I hated my boss" or "I didn't like the people I was working with." Still other folks have told us that they didn't agree with the way their last company worked or did business.

Leadership styles tend to vary between industries and between companies in those industries, *as does almost everything else we've discussed so far*. In fact, we'll stop right here just to make this point: Every company in every field is different and unique. That's the reason we've written this book. There are so many different employers and different ways to work out there that you *have* to know what you're looking for before you hit the job market. Otherwise, you'll simply react, taking the next job offer that seems OK. Leadership and working styles are no different. This chapter will help you determine which ways of working work best for you.

## Leadership Styles

*What kind of leadership works best for you?* If you like and respect the people you work for, you'll obviously be much happier in your job. You'll be more successful, too. We've found that the quality of work and length of tenure really improve when people enjoy working for their boss. Styles of leadership, though, can vary widely, based on what's needed in a certain field and the personality of the leader. In combat, for instance, a friendly pat on the back may need to take a back seat to a shouted order. Most of us won't be in combat any time soon, but the point is an important one.

## What's Out There

*What sorts of leadership styles are out there?* What kind of boss are you looking for? Do you want a friend, a coach, or a mentor? Do you need a taskmaster? Do you want to be pushed or left alone? What sorts of leadership styles have worked well for you in the past? There as many different styles of leadership as the people who are in positions of power, but bosses do tend to divide into a few recognizable categories:

- **The Friend:** A boss who's "just one of the guys." Or gals. This kind of leader will mingle with his or her employees, working right alongside frontline workers, the kind of person who will eat lunch with team members. Relationships are relaxed and almost equal, and the boss/employee part of the equation is really sort of kept on the back burner. This sort of relationship can be great, but it does have its drawbacks—sometimes when the boss really needs to step up and take charge, the overly relaxed nature of the friendship/leadership relationship can be a barrier.

# LEADERSHIP AND WORKING STYLES

- **The Coach:** This kind of leader really is a lot like the traditional athletic coach, a back-slapper and "way-to-goer." The relationship established between the boss and employees is similar to a coach/team relationship, as well, though there are many different dynamics, just as there are in sports coaching situations. Some "teams" will really like and admire their coach and want to work hard for him or her, some will simply perform out of respect, and some will work harder out of fear. The team mentality is key here, as the coach will be leading his or her employees through tasks in a goal-oriented manner. A nice sense of camaraderie can be developed here, though in some situations the "team" idea can be taken a bit too far.

- **The Mentor:** The mentoring relationship between boss and employee can take on an almost parental feel, in that the leader will use his or her past experiences and knowledge to guide younger or greener employees through the corporate gauntlet. The mentor may be a bit more standoffish than the above examples, but he or she will be right there when employees need help, for one-on-one discussions, meetings, lunches, and guidance, as the need arises. The mentor may also be more willing to let employees work through problems themselves in order to find solutions.

- **The Taskmaster:** Don't be frightened off by this sort of leader just because he or she pushes you. Sometimes we all need a little push to get the rock started up the hill. Be wary of someone who's *always* looking over your shoulder or breathing down your neck, but don't shy away from a leadership situation where a boss is usually making sure that things are getting done. Performance and achievement levels can be quite high under a boss who is a taskmaster even some of the time.

- **The Traditional Boss:** A tall guy in a three-piece, charcoal-gray suit who only comes out of his corner office to bark at his employees to "have that on my desk first thing in the morning" is basically a dinosaur in today's workforce. No one remembers the images of smoke-filled rooms or shouted, closed-door meetings fondly. Remember this trend: As the workforce is changing, so, too, are leadership styles. You don't have to settle for working for someone you don't like or respect.

There may not be one right way to work, or even one right boss for you. The best boss displays a combination of leadership styles—she's friendly when she can be, and she's the driving force behind meeting deadlines when she needs to be. He's down in the pit with his people, encouraging them to excel, yet far enough away to let them solve their own problems. Your next leader *can* be a friend *and* a teacher.

### HOT TIP

Look for articles and interviews with leaders of organizations you're considering. While that won't be all you'll need to get an idea of what kind of leaders their people might be, it's a good start.

## Formality

*How formal do you want your relationship with your boss to be?* The following question is really the same sort as above, but it's one worth thinking about: Do you want someone who's a friend as well as a leader, a person who you can call by his or her first name, a person you could see socially? Or are you looking for someone a bit more distant, a bit more

# LEADERSHIP AND WORKING STYLES          61

reserved, someone who will command a different sort of authority and respect? This answer is certainly something you should have in mind as you are mulling over potential employment situations.

## YOUR JOB SEARCH

- As you are looking at various employment opportunities, look at how the people who work there behave. If they are joking and laughing a lot, this relaxed environment is likely to reflect a less formal leadership style in that company. Likewise, if they are industrious and busy all the time, a different sort of leadership style may be in evidence. The working atmosphere usually reflects the attitudes of the leaders.

## Sizing Up Your Boss

*How can you tell if you will respect your new boss just from meeting him or her in an interview?* Unfortunately, you probably can't. There will always be a certain risk involved in taking a new position with a company, and it *can* be a little scary: Will I like my boss? Will he treat me well? Will she teach me what I need to know? The best thing to do is to trust your instincts—you'll meet (or you certainly should meet) the people you'll be working for if you get far enough into the interview process, so once you've spoken to them, trust your gut feel. If you can, you should also try to talk with the people who work for him or her about that person's leadership style. We can't say enough about how important the leader/employee relationship can be to your job satisfaction.

> **REAL-WORLD PRACTICES**
>
> The primary factor affecting a decision to leave an organization is whether or not the manager develops a trusting relationship with the employee. Mastery Works, Inc., Annandale, Virginia, revealed this information during a survey of 500 professionals. Over 95 percent of the respondents chose their relationship with their boss over pay and benefits. Other factors gaining over 90 percent response were the integrity of the manager, work-life balance, and career opportunities.[1]

## Accessibility

*How accessible do you need your boss to be?* Again, all of these questions are really interrelated, but the question of accessibility is an important one. Do you need to be able to approach your boss at any time to discuss issues or problems? Are you happier with someone who is out on the floor with his or her people, sleeves rolled up and doing the work, just like everyone else? Or are you more comfortable with someone who is a little further out of reach, someone who commands a bit more traditional authority? Any or all (or any combination) of these styles are very likely available to you, depending upon what companies you are considering.

Some ways leaders have become more accessible to their employees in the most forward-thinking companies include hot-line telephones that ring directly in the boss's office, a line that he or she answers personally when possible; personal voice mail; personal e-mail addresses; regularly scheduled meetings and sometimes meals with *all employees*; full-company town-meeting–type gatherings in which employees can air concerns, and many other ways of communicating more directly with their people. Ask employers what lines of communication exist between employees and management.

# LEADERSHIP AND WORKING STYLES 63

> **REAL-WORLD PRACTICES**
>
> Special messages sent by CEO Larry Bossidy help Allied Signal's employees located at various plants stay in touch with his vision for the company. Called "Larry's Letters," these e-mail and ink-on-paper messages clearly communicate Bossidy's plans and the importance he places on each individual worker. Employees feel more in touch with Allied and know where the company is headed, plus they feel more connected to the CEO himself, which has been rare in too many corporate environments.[2]

> **REAL-WORLD PRACTICES**
>
> Patricia Gallup is the acclaimed CEO of PC Connection, the computer mail-order firm in Wilmington, Ohio. Gallup does not manage from her office, but rather often chooses to be out on the floor, close to her marketing, engineering, and sales departments.
>
> Gallup is not only visible, but approachable as well. Her people know they can really talk with her about any concern or issue. This kind of closeness really helps everyone at PC Connection feel like part of the team, and they know that Gallup is right there, working just as hard as they are.[3]

## Making Friends

*Do you want a personal relationship with your boss?* No, we don't mean that you have to go to fancy dinners with her once a week, or keep track of how his kids are doing in school, but many people prefer to have at least some personal connection with their bosses. In fact, knowing about how his kids are doing and letting her know about your vacation plans may be just what you're looking for. If you have a kind of friendship with the people you work for, you may find it easier to work for them and more rewarding to work harder.

It's not impossible to find the sort of situation where you can have a friendship with the people you work for, without having a relationship that carries over outside of the workplace. Something as simple as celebrating special occasions can go a long way; we all like to have our birthdays recognized, for instance, and a simple card from your boss can go a long way.

> **REAL-WORLD PRACTICES**
>
> Mary Kay Ash, the founder of Mary Kay Cosmetics in Dallas, Texas, knows that her people appreciate her attention to special occasions. They tell her so. She personally signs every birthday and anniversary card sent to her employees. She also recognizes other special occasions.
>
> New babies receive little silver banks in the shape of ducks. She acknowledges weddings with silver bowls. Employees receive free lunches (for two) or free movie tickets on their birthdays. Plus, employees receive a $100 savings bond for every five years of service.[4]

Did your boss personally sign birthday cards at your last job?

### YOUR JOB SEARCH
- Find out what's going on out there! Ask your friends and colleagues about their relationships with their bosses. Listen for things you'd like and things that might grate on you.

## Taking Responsibility

*How much responsibility are you looking for?* Do you want a lot of space to do your own work, to solve your own problems? Would you prefer an environment in which most tasks are assigned to you? Decide how much responsibility you *want* and how much responsibility you *need* before you begin your search. Job requirements and freedoms are different from company to company, so you'll want to know pretty clearly what you're looking for.

> **HOT TIP**
>
> Are you familiar with a product or service of the company you're considering? Ask how the process and product came about; that is, dig for answers about how the idea was generated and how the product or service was born. You'll find out how new ideas move through the company.

## Openness to Change

*How much do you value openness to change?* Are you an "ideas person"? Do you want the freedom to suggest new ideas in your next job? Have you been frustrated in the past by a company's slow reaction to marketplace conditions or its inability to implement new and better processes? Look for a situation where you'll be free to offer up new ideas, a situation in which your plans and thoughts will be valued and considered. Employees, after all—those closest to any given situation—usually know the most about how to do things better and how to do things right. Most forward-looking companies not only accept employee suggestions, but also encourage them.

> **REAL-WORLD PRACTICES**
>
> To solicit ideas for his new employee-oriented policies, CDW (a company in Vernon Hills, Illinois) CEO Michael Krasny gave every employee five stamped envelopes, addressed to him. The ideas he received helped him to quadruple sales over the past five years. Employees are also impressed that Krasny is not afraid to stack boxes with his people in the warehouse when they need his help.[5]

## Working Styles

*What sort of working styles best suit you?* There are as many working styles as there are leadership styles. Some organizations allow employees to work on their own, some work through traditional "corporate ladder" structures, some have employees work in teams, and some even set up "minicompanies" within the larger corporation. Do you have in mind the ways in which you work best, the ways in which you have been most successful in the past? Some working environments work best for certain kinds of people, and some do not. Know and understand which styles and situations work best for you and you'll be better equipped to seek out what you want.

## Promotions

*What kind of promotional situation are you looking for?* How soon will you want to move up in your new job? What kinds of promotions will you be looking for? Do you want the ability to transfer not just vertically within the organization, but laterally as well? There is no taboo on questioning employers about opportunities to move up and throughout the organization, both in terms of responsibility and benefits. Employers, in fact, will be pleased to discover that you have your eye on moving up in their company or expanding your horizons.

# LEADERSHIP AND WORKING STYLES

> **HOT TIP**
>
> Ask the person you speak to in the initial interview process about his or her history with the company. Has that person moved "up the ladder"? What about other folks in the organization? How often does the organization promote its own to management levels? These answers will help you get a handle on how promotions work in any given company.

## Workplace Politics

*Do you hate workplace politics, too?* It seems like everyone says they hate corporate politics these days. If that's true, though, then why is the idea of "office politics" still so prevalent? This question can be a difficult issue, and one that you might be wary of asking about in an interview or an informational meeting. The reputation of a company may be the best way to go here, in that if a company is riddled with political backstabbing and the like, it will have that sort of reputation among workers throughout the industry. Ask around, but be prudent about how you do so.

## SUMMARY

Finding the right leadership and working styles can be tricky business, since you will only have a complete idea of how things will work *after* you've been in the company for a while. Our best advice to you is to ask as many questions as you can of the people you would be working for, and, if possible, of the people you'd be working with. Have as clear an idea as you can of the way you'd like to feel around your boss and your coworkers before you begin your job search. That way, you'll be more likely to find a good fit.

## ASK YOURSELF:
## Leadership and Working Styles

- What kind of boss am I looking for?
- What leadership styles have worked best for me in the past? What hasn't worked at all?
- Why did I like my previous boss? Why did I dislike him/her?
- Do I need a friend as a leader? A coach? A mentor? Someone who will really crack down on me and push me to get the job done? Does the idea of the traditional boss make my skin crawl, or is it not so bad?
- How formal a relationship do I want with the people I work for?
- What clues should I be looking for when I meet the people I'll be working for that might help me learn what it would be like to work for them?
- Do the people who already work there seem happy in their jobs?
- How accessible do I need my boss to be? Will he or she take my ideas seriously? My concerns?
- What level of friendship makes me most comfortable in terms of my boss?
- How much responsibility do I want/need in my next job?
- How open is the company going to be to initiating change and/or new ideas—mine or anyone else's?
- What kind of working environment am I looking for? What suits me best? How do I work best? Will this company give me the chance to work that way?
- How soon will I be promoted? How soon do I want to be promoted? What are the jobs like above the one I'm applying for? Do those appeal to me as well?
- Is the company working to eliminate office politics as best it can?
- Do I like the people I've spoken to on the phone or in person?

1. *Talent 2000—Retention and Development for Managers*, Mastery Works, Annandale, Virginia, July 28, 1999.
2. "100 Best Companies," *FORTUNE*, January 11, 1999, 140–141.
3. Esther Wachs Book, "Leadership for the Millennium," *Working Woman*, March 1998, 31.
4. Robert Levering and Milton Moskowitz, *The 100 Best Companies to Work For in America*, (New York:Penguin Books, 1994): 269–270.
5. "100 Best Companies," *FORTUNE*, January 11, 1999, 130.

# LEADERSHIP AND WORKING STYLES

## NOTES

Were there any questions in the leadership checklist that stood out to you? Were there any sections in the leadership chapter that struck you as particularly important or especially relevant to your search? Was there something you feel you should jot down now for later reference? Use this space to record your impressions, your ideas, your wants, and your needs in regard to the sort of leadership you'll be looking for.

# 7

# Working Environment

As we work through the options available to you in today's market, it seems logical at this point that we should address the actual working environment. Once you have decided upon the kind of company you're looking for, the type of culture, and the style of leadership, making decisions about what sort of working environment you're looking for is a good next step.

Things to think about in regard to your working environment include the way the office feels and looks, what sort of workspace layout there is and/or could be, where in the building or on the floor you'd be working, where your job is located relative to your home, what sort of benefits in terms of location there are (shopping, food, proximity to commuting choices), workplace safety, facilities, and equipment quality. These are just a few of the choices available to you. We'll use this chapter to explore some of the things you might consider looking for in your next working environment.

## Location, Location, Location

*What aspects of location are important to you?* If what Realtors say *is* true—that the only three things that really matter are location, location, and location—then where the company is *physically*, and not just in the industry rankings, will be a significant factor in making your choice. Where, exactly, would you like to work? Would you be willing to move or to transfer, or are you looking to stay in the community where you are right now? How important is location within a city to you? Are you looking to work downtown or in the suburbs? Do you need to be able to see trees from your window? Do you need a window? Would you consider telecommuting?

These are the sorts of questions you must ask yourself about location. In some instances, where a company is located can be the final deciding factor in a job search. As your search narrows, even if location isn't right up at the top of your list, you can use it to help eliminate some of your choices to put you closer to deciding about your next job.

### YOUR JOB SEARCH

- Is there a specific area where you'd like to work? Begin your job search there. Local newspapers and even smaller community newspapers often have job listings specific to areas as small as neighborhoods or boroughs. Some larger companies may have more than one office or store in your city as well, and you may have choices in terms of which branch or building you'd prefer.
- Is working downtown important to you? Looking for a job in the 'burbs? Limit your search in that way in order to alleviate some of that initial "Want Ad Shock": "I can't believe there are so many jobs out there! I don't even know where to start!"
- Drive through neighborhoods and areas you'd prefer to work in, and just look for "Help Wanted" signs. Don't let the signs limit your thinking. Remember, you may be able to create your own job.

# WORKING ENVIRONMENT

> **HOT TIP**
>
> Want to work in an office, but need to escape to some greenspace every now and then? Many of the new "corporate campus" developments synthesize high-rise office environments with parklike settings; groves of trees, ponds, and even nature and hiking trails may be situated close by.

## Getting There

*What commuting options do you need?* For some people, commuting and transportation can be the key factor in choosing employment. Whether you own your own car and are looking for free parking, or need access to public transportation close by, the way you get to work is certainly something to think about.

Once you've contacted a company, you can ask locational questions about aspects such as proximity to major highways, proximity to public transportation, parking options, and even nearby housing options. If public transportation is important to you, make sure to ask not only about train service (if there is a subway in your town) and bus service, but find about how far a walk it is from the office to the bus stop or train station. Ask about parking costs and options, too. Some companies will pay for downtown parking, if necessary, and many will subsidize garage costs. For those without cars, do not necessarily write off an organization just because they aren't located close to public transportation routes—some companies have even gone so far as to offer company van service either to and from employees' homes or to and from bus and train terminals.

### HOT TIP

Are you really committed to where you live right now? If not, you might consider moving closer to where you will be working to simplify your commuting dilemmas. Some corporations have agreements with apartment management firms nearby and can offer special services or discounts, and in some preplanned corporate communities, housing is offered along with the job either as part of a compensation package or at a reduced rate in a benefits package.

### HOT TIP

Like to be able to walk or ride your bike to work? Inquire about trails and bike paths near the office. You should also ask about where you could change clothes and/or store your bike at work. Some companies give bonuses to employees who pedal or walk to work.

## Flextime

*What sort of flexibility would most benefit you?* Flexibility is one of those words thrown around these days that can mean almost anything. In this context, we mean flexibility in terms of when you work and the time you must be *at* work. Time is becoming more and more important as a benefit in today's marketplace, and we'll discuss that in greater detail in coming chapters, but time is also an important part of the working environment in all its forms.

## WORKING ENVIRONMENT 75

- **Traditional flextime:** The most traditional forms of flextime involve such working options as choosing shifts and work schedules, choosing to work on, say Saturday, as opposed to one of the regular workweek days, or changing the traditional nine to five schedule to more adequately suit your needs.

- **Home/office flextime:** With the rise of newer and faster technologies, more and more people are able to work from home with greater efficiency and success. The time you actually have to be in the office may be less than you think.

- **The virtual office:** Like above, but with the home/office balance even more heavily weighted to the home and travel options. E-mail, fax capabilities, videoconferencing, and audioconferencing technologies, and Internet and intranet advances make working in the traditional office setting less and less mandatory.

Ask about flextime and virtual office options when you are discussing work schedules and time requirements. You should also find out what sort of arrangements the company has worked out with employees in the past.

---

### REAL-WORLD PRACTICES

Motek, a software developer located in Beverly Hills, California, represents the best work option we've discussed so far in this chapter. Since Motek is located in the land of giant freeways that often seem like parking lots, CEO Ann Price jumped on the idea of telecommuting. What happened surprised her (and us). She often visited her employees in their home offices and was taken aback with what she observed. Many of her employees had pictures of other Motek employees on their desks.

*continued*

Few employees, including Price, came into the office on a daily basis, so the office space was small. Yet the office was used as a hub and the location of their monthly meetings, and Price wanted employees to have their own desks whenever they needed to be there. Within a year, almost all of the employees had relocated closer to the office and were coming in on a daily basis. They enjoyed working with each other.

Price was not concerned about her telecommuting employees working enough. She was concerned about their working too much. She knows that life balance is an important element to having happy, productive employees.

Motek's corporate culture supports people walking to work. One of their employees who used to commute at least two hours on the freeway each day now lives one block from the office and walks to work. She believes the quality of her life has substantially improved. The company also helps find housing for any employee who wishes to abandon the Los Angeles freeways and walk to work.[1]

## Work/Life Balance

*What is work/life balance, and what does it mean to you?* Work/life balance is a term we use to discuss the actual balance between your work life and your home life. Stop and think about this question for a minute: how many waking hours do you spend at your job, and how many waking hours do you spend at home? The hypercompetitive business world naturally is driving the number of work hours up, and that's not always a bad thing, but we're worried (and we're not the only ones) that the amount of time people spend at home is decreasing.

Of course you want to work hard and move up the corporate ladder. Your employer wants you to succeed, too. However, as the competitive balance has shifted away from the employers (they were much more "in charge" when there were fewer jobs and more folks seeking those jobs) to the

# WORKING ENVIRONMENT

workers (now companies can't fill all the jobs they have), most managers have backed off of the immense time requirements of past decades. They allow (in some cases, encourage) a greater equity in work/life balance. You may not have to turn in twelve-hour days to move onward and upward.

You have a life. You may have a dog who needs a little quality tennis-ball time, a family who needs all sorts of quality everything from you all the time, or simply a good book to get home to. Take back your life, at least a little bit. If a better work/life balance is important to you, then ask about work hours and flexibility options when pursuing available jobs.

### HOT TIP

Is time at home one of the most important aspects in your job search decision? If you're willing to forego some benefits that come with full-time employment, you might consider seeking contract rather than salaried employment. Actual office time requirements are likely to decrease. We should warn you that this type of employment can be far less secure and may not result in the highest possible compensation and benefits packages, but if you want to control your own time, this option may be the way to go.

## Physical Environment

*What about the way the office actually looks and feels is important to you?* The physical environment in which you work *is* important; there's no doubt about it. How things look and feel can be really key in determining your comfort level at work. Think about just some of the smallest things for a moment.

- Would you be allowed to have a plant on your desk? Photos of the family?

- What colors are the walls and carpet? Is that OK with you? (Don't laugh here . . . well, you can, that's fine, but keep reading—color in the workplace is no small detail. If yellow gives you a headache, you might be wary of working in a place with yellow walls or even yellow molding.) Consider the amount of time you spend choosing colors in your own home. You probably won't get to pick the colors of your next office or place of work, but you can certainly choose against them.

- How busy is the environment? If, for instance, you don't like a lot of stimuli all at once, retail may not be for you.

- Do you need to be able to close an office door to shut out the world every now and then? To enjoy some quiet to get work done?

- Would you get to hang things on the walls?

- Do you want to be a "Cubicle Creature"? Remember—some cubicle offices are just like the ones lampooned in cartoon strips, and some aren't. Don't be scared off simply because of the existence of cubicles, though you might be a bit more wary!

- Do you need to be near a window? A door?

### HOT TIP
Many offices are trending away from traditional, stuffy corporate milieu toward a more homelike environment. If this sort of environment appeals to you, look for sofas, plants, break rooms, and comfortable working conditions when you go in for your interview.

# WORKING ENVIRONMENT

## And Now for Something Completely Different

*Are you looking for something completely different?* We've already discussed this in previous chapters, but as more and more companies are trying to simultaneously attract employees and improve productivity, some are trying radical new ways of working. You do not have to accept the traditional office setups anymore. Figure out how you work best and how you'd like to work, and look for a company that does business that way.

### REAL-WORLD PRACTICES

Bob Noble, president and CEO of Noble & Associates, the largest advertising agency in the country that's devoted to the food industry, calls his firm, "a company that the client built." Noble believes that the open architecture layout of his offices is a reflection of their client focus. Open architecture refers to an office layout that abandons most of the traditional set pieces, such as walls and partitions, for larger workspaces where everyone can see and work with everyone else.

In order to keep clients ahead of the changing marketplace, Noble realized his company needed to be more nimble, get work done more quickly, and shorten the time between project inception and completion. They also needed to provide the same services for less money and deliver more value. Oh, and one more thing—he wanted to keep his employees on their toes, interested, and happy.

Using the metaphor of the solar system, the organization eliminated layers of management and divided the company into teams. Its teams all have astronomical names like The Milky Way, Mercury, Venus, and Saturn. Serving all the other heavenly bodies is Earth, which includes Information Technology, Accounting, Human Resources, and other "universal" services to all the teams.

*continued*

Basically, the company created a group of small agencies to offer an umbrella of services; now the quality client teams offer one-stop shopping. The smaller agencies have more people with broader talents, so they've reduced the number of steps and improved processes to shorten completion time. There's no more traffic department, for instance; each team handles its own traffic. This arrangement actually gets more employees involved more of the time.

To support the teams' working arrangements, Noble developed an office layout that is so flexible that it can be reconfigured within minutes to allow groups of employees to collaborate or work independently. There are no walls. All partitions and desks are on wheels; all phone jacks and outlets are in the floor. Each "planet space" has two to four conference rooms and one to two telephone booths to allow complete privacy for personal calls. Of course, comfortable congregate spaces that promote collaboration and creativity are an important aspect of this design.

Nobel encourages "intrapreneuring" among his employees, allowing the teams to buy the services of other team members at "inside" rates, when the employees are not otherwise occupied with their own clients' work.

Of course, their gain-sharing program has an astronomical name, too—"Comet Pay." To foster teamwork, Comet Pay is only distributed when the entire solar system has reached its assigned threshold of profitability.

Is it working? In fact, the new system is exceeding expectations. The clients are happy and so are the employees. They're working in a system that's new, that works better, and that's more fun.[2]

# WORKING ENVIRONMENT

## Hideouts

*How important are break areas to you? Eating opportunities? Areas where you can get away?* Like a lot of other questions, these can most easily be answered by looking around the place where you're thinking about working. Ask someone to show you the facilities, and make sure that you're not just seeing the offices or the floor. Ask to see the coffee machine! After all (and of course this is just a very small example), you just can't get by without access to good coffee, right?

Other things to consider are proximity to restaurants, in-house cafeterias, whether or not the company caters lunch for employees from time to time, and how comfortable, accessible, and available the break rooms are.

As we revert to a more electronic culture in America, people are valuing their "outside time" more and more highly. If you need to be able to get outside and stand somewhere where you can't hear or smell the highway, then be sure to include that on your list of needs.

### YOUR JOB SEARCH

- Ask the people who answer the phone at whatever company you might be considering what they do to get away during the workday. They may let you in on a great escape you hadn't thought of, or they may help you direct your search elsewhere.

> **REAL-WORLD PRACTICES**
>
> Gymboree, located in Burlingame, California, designs, manufactures, and retails a complete line of children's fashion apparel, accessories, and play products. They market those products exclusively through their own nearly 500 corporate-owned and managed stores in the US, Canada, and the United Kingdom.
>
> About a year ago now, Gymboree began a once-a-week program of "corporate recess." Every Thursday at 3 P.M., a bell sounds over the public address system. Recess lasts for 20 minutes. Their campus sports a lake with a walking area and hopscotch is available. The purpose is for employees to spend a few minutes together outside of the work environment catching up with one another, getting some fresh air and exercise, further creating a sense of team.
>
> Each Wednesday at 3 P.M., Gymboree also provides snack time for its employees. This break also lasts for about 20 minutes, during which time workers come together in a central location to munch on the snacks that range from chips and salsa to cookies and milk.
>
> These two corporate benefits reflect the company's "celebrate childhood" philosophy and are only two of the myriad family-friendly benefits Gymboree offers.[3]

## Facilities

*What are you looking for in terms of facilities?* Do you want to work with the latest equipment? Do you like to have a lot of space to work? Need access to the latest technologies? Think back over your past jobs to get a handle about what you liked about the physical aspects of your job, and what you didn't like as well, and then you'll be armed with the information you need to find exactly what you want.

> **HOT TIP**
>
> Find out about the safety record of any company you're considering. No one wants to work in an unsafe environment. Watchdog organizations like the Better Business Bureau can either provide you with the information you need or tell you where to go to get it. Put safety at the top of your job-search criteria list.

## A Roof over Your Head

*Do you want to work inside or outside?* Another easy question, right? It's another important one, too. If you are the kind of person who needs to be outside, don't take a job in, say, accounting. Or, look for a firm that would let you use your accounting skills in an alternative environment; a landscaping company might need an on-site cost manager, for instance.

## Friends and Family

*What sort of social environment do you need? What level of family involvement are you looking for?* Great employers recognize the value of involving employees' families in their work lives. Family-friendly events like picnics, parties, trips to amusement parks and ball games, and company public service projects are only a few of the ways companies are reaching out not just to workers, but to workers' families.

Quality employers also provide flexibility for time needs in terms of family events and occasions such as weddings, birthdays, and anniversaries. These companies will also be understanding in times of crisis, such as illness or death in employees' immediate families. Ask about family-friendly policies when researching organizations.

### REAL-WORLD PRACTICES

Emerson Electric in St. Louis has a big Christmas party, mostly for the children of their employees. This gala event features face painters, fortune tellers, an interactive magician, and entertainers who sing children's songs. But the most fun activity for the children is the cake decorating activity. Kids get to decorate their own small cakes, then take them home.[4]

### REAL-WORLD PRACTICES

HMOs traditionally have not been considered optimal places to work. That was before United Healthcare. The Greensboro, North Carolina office provides some unusual benefits for its employees. At Halloween, not only do the employees dress up, but also the children of the employees come trick or treating in the office. The employees pay for the candy, and the company provides prizes for the best costumes.[5]

### REAL-WORLD PRACTICES

Every summer, Texas Instruments holds a camp for employees' children at its Dallas headquarters fitness facility. Begun in 1995, the Summer Time Kids Camp served approximately 100 children, ages five to eleven, in 1998. The eleven-week program, which costs $100 per child per week, runs from 7 A.M. to 6 P.M., Monday through Friday, and provides hot lunches and weekly field trips for the children. The camp is run by Bright Horizons Family Solutions, a national, corporate childcare company.

## Jeans or Ties?

*How important is the formality of the workplace in your decision?* Do you love to dress up? Do you only feel at home in blue jeans? Many offices have gone to a more casual dress code, and some have gone full-time casual unless an important client is in the office. Retail and sales positions usually have specific dress-code requirements you should be aware of. It may seem like a small aspect of your decision, but consider this: the level of formality in your workplace will influence the way you feel about your job before you even get out of bed in the morning.

### HOT TIP

Don't dress down for your interview. However, while you're there, have a look at what everyone else is wearing. Ask about dress code. Don't let something sneak up on you!

## SUMMARY

As with any of these criteria, make sure that "what they say" matches up with "what they do."

Be entirely convinced that the company you are considering is not just paying lip service to issues of environment. You will have to work every day, so be sure that where you work makes you feel happy and satisfied.

## ASK YOURSELF: Workplace

- What aspects of location make a difference to me? Do I want to work downtown? Uptown? In the suburbs? In a rural area? Do I want to be out of the office every day? Do I want to travel?
- What transportation issues are important to me? What matters—proximity to interstates, avoiding traffic and gridlock, proximity to public transportation, distance from home?
- Do I want to be able to ride my bike or walk to work?
- Would I be willing to move? Transfer?
- What do I need in terms of schedule? Hours per week?
- Can I/do I want to telecommute? Work at satellite work sites?
- What sort of work/life balance am I looking for? How much must I be at work? How much do I need to be at home?
- What do I want the office to look like?
- Do I need an office? Can I work in a cubicle?
- How would I be able to personalize my workspace?
- How would I be working? In teams? Alone? In my office? Do I want something like open architecture or floating workstations?
- What would I be able to do to get away? What do the break areas look like? Where would I eat lunch? Could I bring my own? Would I have to eat at my desk? How long are the breaks?
- What kind of facilities do I need or want? Will this company offer the latest equipment and technology?
- Where would I be working: at a desk, outside, on the third floor, the thirtieth? Are there windows? Would I have to work standing?
- Will I have to wear Armani suits? Wranglers? Flip-flops? Is there a uniform? Can I wear a ball cap? A mustache?
- Does "what they say" match up with "what they do"? With "what I see"?

1. Roger Herman and Joyce Gioia, *Lean & Meaningful* (Winchester, VA: Oakhill Press, 1998), 74–76.
2. Interview with Bob Noble, December 17, 1999.
3. Joyce Gioia, "Too stressed-out to work? Enjoy recess and snack times when you work for Gymboree," *The Workforce Stability Alert* (August, 1999): 8.
4. Interview with Dick Hall, December 16, 1999.
5. Joyce Gioia, "Celebrate with Children," *The Workforce Stability Alert* (April 2000): 5.

# WORKING ENVIRONMENT

## NOTES

Were there any questions in the environment checklist that stood out to you? Were there any sections in the environment chapter that struck you as particularly important or especially relevant to your search? Was there something you feel you should jot down now for later reference? Use this space to record your impressions, your ideas, your wants, and your needs in regard to the sort of environment you'll be looking for.

# 8

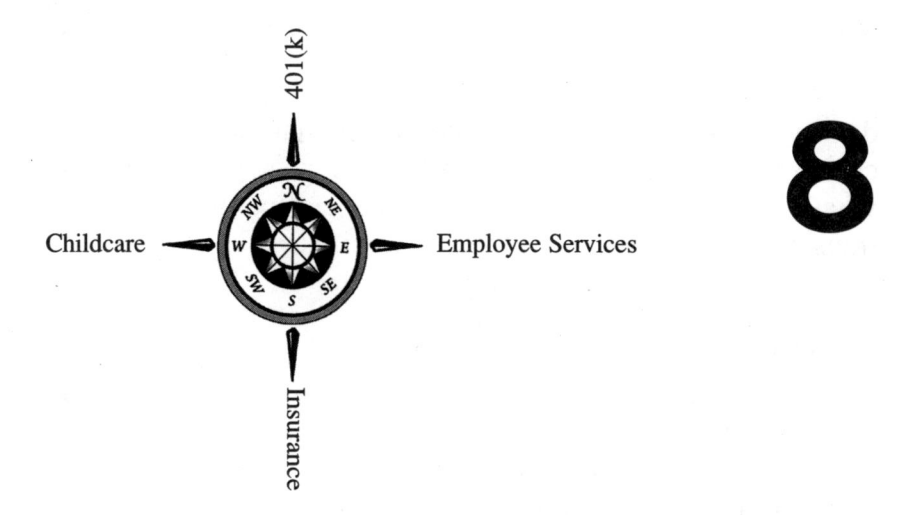

# Benefits

Those little numbers on your paycheck mean a lot; there's no doubt about it. And don't worry—we'll talk about compensation and pay in the next chapter. While money is necessary, we know it's not the only factor. If you're like the majority of people, it's not the most important thing, either. We've already discussed things like quality leadership and the value of the company itself, as well as specific work environments and cultures. We know that money in the bank isn't the only factor affecting your decision.

Employers are getting more and more creative with the benefits they are offering their employees. For the sake of clarity, we'll refer to benefits as any of the perks or bonuses of working for a specific company that are not strictly paycheck-related. Happy employees stay at their jobs longer. Employers know that, and are doing everything they can to satisfy their employees and make their workers' lives easier. Yes—traditional benefits like insurance and retirement are still very much in place, and, in fact, we'll begin our discussion with those—but as the labor market tightens for employers, the benefits packages have grown far beyond what workers could expect just one generation ago. The options available to you are almost unlimited.

### Insurance Choices

*What insurance options are you looking for?* The most common benefit for full-time employees, and perhaps the most important, is health insurance. This benefit has become practically universal with the advent of HMOs and other non-traditional health-care provider organizations. In addition to regular catastrophic coverage, however, employers' options have become increasingly more varied, and, as a result, so have yours. Even if a certain service is not available in an employer's plan, it may be available to you at a lowered rate in an added payment or "piggyback" plan. Some of the many options available to you are as follows:

- **Hospitalization and major medical:** This coverage is, or should be, essentially universal for full-time employees (we'll cover part-time employees at the end of this section). As a benefit free of charge to you, your employer should provide this sort of high-level catastrophic insurance. Accident or injury as well as major illness requiring hospitalization are covered in this plan. While you hopefully will never have to use this service, it can really serve as a "peace of mind" benefit—you won't be facing huge bills if you break your leg rollerblading or tear up your knee at your daughter's father-daughter soccer game. It frees you to live your life a bit more easily.

- **Routine health:** Most employers provide some type of paid or copaid routine "maintenance" health insurance. We're talking about plans in which for, say, ten dollars, you can go to the doctor for lesser illnesses or routine exams. This benefit has become very nearly universal as

# BENEFITS

well, at least to the point where you should be able to see the doctor a few times a year at low cost. Look for these type of services when beginning your choice process.

- **Life:** Most of the major hospitalization plans include a life insurance package, though employers can also provide this service (or an enhanced policy) as a group benefit or through a copay or matching pay practice as part of a negotiated benefits package.

- **Dental:** Though many policies do not include dental, copay options may exist on the company's existing policy. As well, you should know that carrying a dental policy for employees is not as expensive as one might think or as some companies believe, and today's progressive employers have begun carrying separate dental packages for their employees. Companies and organizations offering benefits such as dental insurance signal a greater willingness to help their people.

- **Vision:** Vision coverage—even a paid once-a-year eye exam, as ophthalmologist suggest—can be another inexpensive addition to a health plan. Some policies will even pay or copay for glasses and contacts. You should ask about these possibilities when discussing insurance benefits.

- **Other:** There are a variety of other insurance benefits available that don't necessarily relate to physical health. Group automobile insurance may be offered at a lower cost than you could find outside the organization; prepaid legal may be an option in the case of accident or wrongdoing; even such far-out options as insuring against poor weather during a vacation may be available. Ask about inventive or creative insurance options. You may be surprised at what you hear.

- **Pets:** Don't laugh. If you have a dog or cat (Andrew, as a child, took a gerbil and a turtle to the vet at various points), you know that regular health checkups can be expensive, and emergency veterinary care can be exorbitant. Health insurance for pets may be available; group discounts on pet products may be offered as well.

> ### REAL-WORLD PRACTICES
>
> Pet Assure is a pet-care savings program designed to make veterinary—as well as everyday—care more affordable for pet owners. Through a network of participating veterinarians, Pet Assure customers and members save 25 percent on all veterinary products and services. Members can also save 50 percent on pet supplies and other services, like food and grooming. This service is not an insurance program. For more information, visit *www.petassure.com*. You might direct your employer to that Website as well!

## Domestic Partners

*Are domestic-partner benefits an important part of your decision?* According to the U.S. Census Bureau, the number of unmarried-couple households jumped from 1.6 million in 1980 to 4.2 million in 1998. That number is sure to dramatically increase yet again when the results of the 2000 census are in. Whether same-sex or different-sex households, the number of unmarried partners is quite significant in today's marketplace.

Though you must meet certain qualifications, particularly oriented toward confirming interdependence, enlightened companies have begun extending benefits to unmarried partners. Though only a small percentage of companies currently offer this benefit, the trend is growing. Pioneering companies in this effort include Disney, the San Francisco 49ers, and Digital Equipment. Consider what you'll be looking for in terms of social citizenship as you begin looking for your next job.

## Mommies and Daddies

*Will you be seeking maternal/paternal benefits?* Most health insurance plans will cover pregnancies, and some companies have begun offering insurance coverage to adoptive parents and their children, as well. These insurance issues are not the only things to consider, however; paid leave for childcare can be a make-it-or-break-it benefit for many parents. Parental leave has become fairly common for pregnancies, and it is available in some arenas for adoptions as well. Paid and unpaid leave can vary widely, with benefits ranging from full salary for twelve or more weeks to unpaid leave with the promise of holding your job. If you are planning to start or increase a family, make sure you're well versed on the options available to you and the options available at the company you're considering.

### REAL-WORLD PRACTICES

If you were going to adopt a child, wouldn't you like twelve weeks paid leave to bond with your new child? You can get it from the same company that offers 26 weeks of pregnancy leave and pays for childcare while employees are away at industry conferences. The company is PC Connection, a New Hampshire-based mail order distributor of computers that employs over 800 happy people.

The open leadership style of Founder/CEO Patricia Gallup is a significant factor in the company's success. The company has no trouble attracting workers. Why? Competitive wages and full health benefits, even for part-timers. When a housing shortage made it difficult for her to recruit, Gallup initiated a program to build homes and sell them to employees for $40,000 below cost. Employees got free snow tires and windshield wipers so they could safely navigate New Hampshire's winter roads.

*continued*

> Other innovative benefits? Workers can take a one-month leave for any reason, such as caring for elderly family members. How about free turkeys at Thanksgiving, ski jaunts, casino nights, and hiking trips? Even all-expenses-paid vacations to the Bahamas are not unheard of. The most productive salesperson can earn a cruise to Cancun, and Gallup pays a $1,000 cash bounty for attracting a new employee. "Employees are customers, too," says Gallup, "so we have to exceed their expectations." Result: only 4 percent of her employees leave each year. With an employer that takes care of its people like that, would you leave?[1]

## Part-Timers

*Will you be working part-time?* Part-timers in many companies can receive benefits as well: in some, like the previous example, they can receive full health benefits, and in other situations benefits are available at reduced prices. Don't abandon your desire for coverage just because you don't work full-time.

### YOUR JOB SEARCH

- Take a few minutes, sit down at your kitchen table and make a list of health benefits you need. Then make a list of health benefits you want. Your "need" list should be part of your "make-it-or-break-it" decision process, and your "want" list can help you decide between companies. Your "want" list may also be negotiable as part of your overall compensation package.

## Health Benefits

*What health benefits are you seeking beyond insurance?* Many companies are now offering wellness programs beyond

# BENEFITS 95

traditional and even nontraditional insurance programs. Annual physical examinations, smoking cessation programs, and counseling groups may only be part of the package. Some of these newer options are detailed below.

- **Health club memberships:** Some companies have gyms built into their corporate campus; others offer low-cost or no-cost memberships to local fitness clubs. As added benefits, employee tournaments may be routine, physical trainers may be available or on staff, and aerobics or other fitness classes may be offered.

### HOT TIP

Make sure you get to see the gym before you sign on, or before you agree to copay for membership—gym quality varies widely from place to place, and on-site gyms may not be up to par, as far as you are concerned. The quality of the fitness facility may not make the difference between you taking a job offer or not, but it might make a difference in terms of leaving your old gym or signing up to pay for the new one.

- **Nutrition programs:** Even if there is no on-site cafeteria, employers have begun employing nutritionists for company-wide programs or regular seminars. You are of course not required to take these courses or programs, but they may be there for the taking if you're interested.

- **Wellness training:** Employers have begun making experts available to their employees in the fields of stress management, time management, child rearing, and other daily issues. Some also provide, whether through health insurance or other programs, access to therapists and counselors, should the need arise.

## Financial Benefits

*What financial benefits will you be seeking?* Though we'll discuss finance in detail in the next chapter, it is also important to highlight financial benefits here—creative retirement programs, mutual fund access, and unique payment plan options are only a few of the possible pay-related benefits out there. Ask about creative payment and savings plans.

Some employers offer the services of accountants or Certified Financial Planners to employees at a reduced cost or even free. Give serious consideration to employers who care about you enough to support your present and future financial strength.

## Vacations

*What kinds of vacation plans are important to you?* Vacations can be one of the most important aspects of your job. Even if you love your job, love the environment, love the people you work with, and love your boss, you'll still need to get away once in a while. Variations in vacation plans can include amount of time allowed for vacations per year, how that time changes with tenure, and number of sick days and holidays.

---

### REAL-WORLD PRACTICES

Vacations can be a huge bonus. Take, for example, Motek, the software company in Beverly Hills. The CEO, Ann Price, gives each of her employees one month off per year—with pay. Price also gives each employee $5,000, but there is a catch. That $5,000 must be used for airlines, cruises, hotels, and other travel expenses. Employees are expected to take this time off to rest and rejuvenate.

Longer time-off options may be out there for the taking as well. Colleges and universities have long offered sab-

*continued*

# BENEFITS

baticals, and companies are now beginning to follow the trend. These may involve full pay, a stipend of some sort, or simply the promise of the chance to return to your job when the sabbatical period is over. This extended time off may sound far-fetched as a benefit, but you should not hesitate to inquire about these sort of options, particularly at the upper levels of employment.

## REAL-WORLD PRACTICES

Intel began offering sabbaticals in 1969, when the company was founded. Employees who take sabbaticals have an opportunity to reenergize; those who are not on sabbatical have an opportunity to take on new challenges by performing some of the duties normally performed by the recharging employees. Microsoft also offers sabbaticals—as a reward for high-performing employees. Hallmark sponsors team sabbaticals, where three to ten people take some time off to study, learn, and develop new creative skills. American Express allows employees to take a year of paid leave for community service after ten years of service. Dupont employees can take a year of unpaid leave, but keep their health benefits. McDonald's offers eight weeks of paid leave to full-time workers after ten years of service.

## Childcare

*Do you need childcare choices?* More and more employers are offering childcare services for their employees. These services may be on-site with full-time staff members, or services may be contracted through off-site providers like KinderCare or La Petite. In other cases, the care center is off-site, but staffed by the employer or by a consortium of employers. These services may be offered as part of a compensation package or at a reduced rate.

> **REAL-WORLD PRACTICES**
>
> La Petite operates a large childcare facility for employees at Opryland Hotel in Nashville, Tennessee. The Child Development Center is open around the clock to accommodate employees at the convention hotel, known for being the largest in the United States outside Las Vegas. The childcare facility serves 350 children. The hotel subsidizes rates on a sliding scale, so that the most any employee pays is 80 percent of the normal rate charged by La Petite.

## Other Dependent Care

Do you need other dependent care? Care services are expanding to include other dependents of employees, including parents or other children in the home. Though these services may be exceedingly expensive—and in some cases too expensive—for the employer to provide, many at least provide referral services, and some will subsidize care costs.

## Backup Childcare

*Did you know about occasional and backup childcare?* Unforeseen circumstances—like illness or inclement weather—may require "emergency" childcare from time to time. If the kids have to stay home from school due to snow and ice, for instance, you might have to stay home with them. Employers are much more interested in having you on the job, though, and have begun programs to help their employees in these unexpected moments.

> **REAL-WORLD PRACTICES**
>
> At BankBoston, the number of employees registered to use the company's Snowy Day program is growing each year. More than 400 employees are signed up to take
>
> *continued*

# BENEFITS

their children to a safe respite on snow days when schools close. The program is offered at seven BankBoston locations in Massachusetts, Rhode Island, and Connecticut and is free to all 16,000 employees.

At the corporate office in Boston, the Snowy Day program is held in a big, bright conference center on the 35th floor. While BankBoston provides the materials for activities, crafts, and games, as well as a VCR, television, and snacks, the actual oversight of the program is managed by Bright Horizons Family Solutions, Cambridge, Massachusetts.

The program offers employees a safe and clean place to take their children, and allows them to still come to work.

## REAL-WORLD PRACTICES

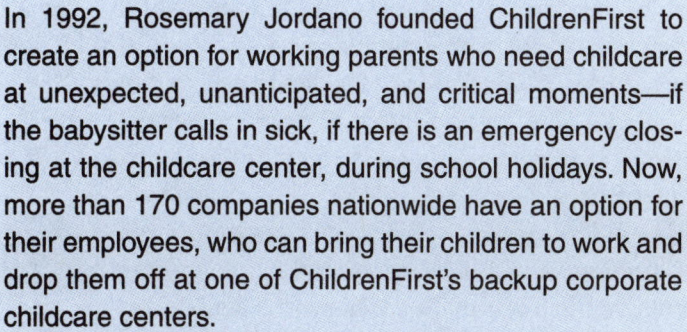

In 1992, Rosemary Jordano founded ChildrenFirst to create an option for working parents who need childcare at unexpected, unanticipated, and critical moments—if the babysitter calls in sick, if there is an emergency closing at the childcare center, during school holidays. Now, more than 170 companies nationwide have an option for their employees, who can bring their children to work and drop them off at one of ChildrenFirst's backup corporate childcare centers.

Clients of ChildrenFirst now include such prominent and varied organizations as Gillette, Conde Nast, Deloitte & Touche, Sara Lee, Colgate-Palmolive, Avon Products, American Express, Chevron, Arco, Skadden, Arps, Slate, and Wells Fargo. Employees of these and other businesses say that having backup childcare is critical to their job satisfaction.

## Cats and Dogs

*Would you like to have pet-care options?* Ever come home to find the sofa unstuffed and strewn around your house? Feel guilty thinking about the cats being lonely or the dog waiting for you in the window? We'll grant you that it might be a little hard to come by yet, but a few companies—and more every year—are offering their employees some sort of pet care. Some employees provide on-site pet care or will subsidize off-site "doggie day care." Some will offer pet care while the employee is traveling on company business. Some, if the environment is right, even allow dogs at work. Imagine being able to bring your pet to work with you!

### REAL-WORLD PRACTICES

When Justice Telecom, at one time the fastest-growing privately held company in the country, first opened its doors over six years ago, its staff members were young and many did not have children. But they did have pets. A number of them had dogs that were just as important to them as children were to other people.

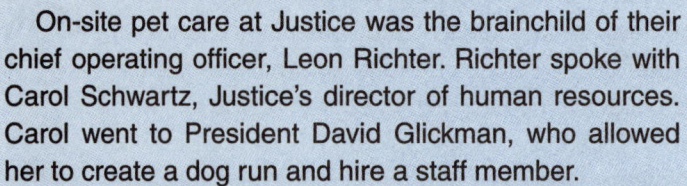

On-site pet care at Justice was the brainchild of their chief operating officer, Leon Richter. Richter spoke with Carol Schwartz, Justice's director of human resources. Carol went to President David Glickman, who allowed her to create a dog run and hire a staff member.

Due to reorganization, Justice needed the space and had to eliminate the dog run. But don't worry: Justice employees still enjoy bringing their pets to work with them. But now, the pets stay under their owners' desks. At lunch, the dog owners take their pets for walks in nearby grassy areas. The mere presence of pets in the office "relieves stress" in their intense environment.

### REAL-WORLD PRACTICES

Pets are welcome at work at Netscape, though there are some strict policies. Dogs may not eat each other's food or have more than two indoor accidents. They must be

*continued*

# BENEFITS

considerate, quiet, and congenial. If a dog misbehaves three times, the owner must take it to obedience school. The owner must show human resource professionals proof that the dog has graduated from obedience school. Ben & Jerry's and Iams, the pet food manufacturer in Dayton, Ohio, also have pet-friendly policies.

## YOUR JOB SEARCH

- Well, it may not be realistic to center your search around pet care. However, as you are looking, ask about the possibility—the company may surprise you and say yes, or you may give them an idea about instituting pet care where there was none before. Like all benefits, you'll never know unless you ask.

## Still More Choices

*What other benefits might interest you?* There are several kinds of benefits that may be industry-specific or company-specific, or perhaps just benefits you hadn't thought of before. We'll run down a quick list, though these are by no means all of the special benefits that are out there.

- **Discounts:** Whether in food service or high-end manufacturing, companies generally offer employee discounts for products and services. If these are important to you—for instance, if you buy a lot of CDs—you might consider looking for a position in the music industry, whether in retail, manufacturing, or management.

- **Logo apparel:** Many companies will give, or sell at reduced prices, clothing and other items with their logo. It's free advertising for the companies, yes, but you also get high-quality items at lower costs.

- **Trade with other companies:** Many organizations have set up trade agreements among a grouping of companies, so that not only their products and services are available at discount rates, but those of other companies as well. Coupon books or membership cards may be given to employees. It's not a huge benefit, but it can be a nice perk.

- **Reward programs:** Some firms will reward top sellers or highly praised customer service people with bonuses, special prizes, or even vacation time. Look into bonus and reward programs, particularly if you are in a "pay for performance"–type situation.

- **Value-added services:** Many companies have begun adding on-site or value-added services to their benefits programs. These may include bringing in tax or accounting specialists to be made available to workers, dry cleaning pickup, car wash and detailing services, massage, shoe repair, tailoring, and barber and beauty services.

- **Transportation:** Some companies may offer transport to and from work; at the highest levels, this perk may mean company cars, and at lower levels, this service may mean van service for those not near public transportation routes.

- **Local perks:** Many companies have season tickets to cultural events like community theater, opera, symphony, and other events, and some also have box seats at local sporting events. Find out about these—seats front-row center at a musical or on the 50-yard-line can be more fun than you think!

---

### REAL-WORLD PRACTICES

One of the unusual perks at Datatel in Fairfax, Virginia, is their Free Ticket Program. Each month, some of their employees get to choose from a healthy selection of venues. From concerts performed by Barbra Streisand, Mary Chapin Carpenter and the National Symphony Orchestra, to sporting events hosted by the Wizards, Orioles,

*continued*

# BENEFITS

and the Redskins, to theater tickets for productions at the Kennedy Center for the Performing Arts, employees enjoy attending these very special events *at no charge*.

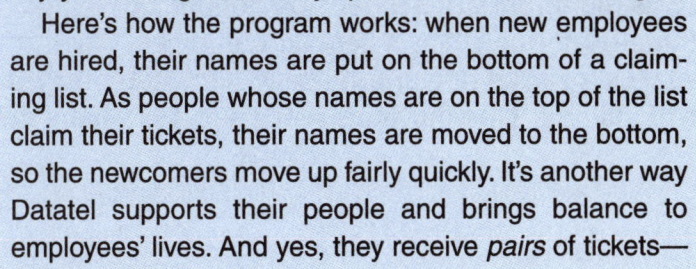

Here's how the program works: when new employees are hired, their names are put on the bottom of a claiming list. As people whose names are on the top of the list claim their tickets, their names are moved to the bottom, so the newcomers move up fairly quickly. It's another way Datatel supports their people and brings balance to employees' lives. And yes, they receive *pairs* of tickets—not just one.

## REAL-WORLD PRACTICES

At The Herman Group in Greensboro, North Carolina, Joyce and Roger support the Greensboro Symphony with subscriptions to both the Classical Series and the Pops concerts. When Joyce and Roger are out of town, which is most of the time, team members use the tickets to take their families.

## HOT TIP

Ask around about what sorts of benefits other companies have, and you'll get an idea about how competitive the company you're considering is in terms of the marketplace as a whole.

## Continuing Education

*Are you looking for educational opportunities?* More employers than you think are willing to pay for college and postgraduate study, particularly if it relates to your work. Employers will also pay for basic study skills, basic math and reading education, and for industry-specific seminars. This tuition assistance is really a terrific benefit, spawned by the need for greater and more diverse knowledge in today's workplace as the information explosion continues.

Everything from English as a Second Language, other foreign languages, or even doctoral management study may be yours for the taking. Do your homework and see what's out there.

## YOUR JOB SEARCH

- You may want to tailor your job search to the kind of education *you're* looking for. If you're interested in pursuing an MBA, a degree for which financial aid is more readily available at large corporations, you may well want to seek out a company that will pay for all or part of your educational costs.

## REAL-WORLD PRACTICES

Ames Rubber, in Hamburg, New Jersey, partnered with a local community college to develop a comprehensive training program in basic skills and English as a Second Language (ESL). Funding from the New Jersey Department of Labor paid the costs for materials and community college instructors; Ames paid for the employees' wages during class time. Classes were held once a week for 13 weeks. Those who needed further training were enrolled for another 13 weeks. The ESL classes are ongoing one-on-one tutoring sessions.

## REAL-WORLD PRACTICES

At CIGNA Group Insurance in Philadelphia, both employees and employer rank education at the top of the benefits list. There are two educational benefit programs: the Education Reimbursement Program is a nationwide effort that pays for employees who have completed undergraduate degrees to obtain advanced degrees.

The other program, more unusual, is the CIGNA-Penn program, through which employees can earn an undergraduate liberal arts degree from the University of Pennsylvania without ever leaving the workplace. Courses are taught by university faculty at company facilities. About 150 people are enrolled in the program, which is really appreciated by employees who have minimal time and resources. The only expenses to the employee-students, who must meet university standards, are for application fees and books.[2]

## SUMMARY

Benefits programs are an exceedingly important aspect of your search for new employment. While the dollars are a big factor, so are the benefits and perks that come with your new job. Some can be a significant aspect of your overall job satisfaction. Those positions don't just *pay* you money, but may *save* you money and present you with new and different opportunities. Think about what you'll be looking for in terms of benefits—before you sit down with a company to discuss employment—and you may be able to negotiate or even change policy. Also, be sure to listen to what they have to offer. They may have benefits you hadn't even considered.

## ASK YOURSELF: Benefits

- What insurance options are most important to me? What do I need, and what do I want? Dental? Eye care? Maternal? Other options?
- Do I need or want auto insurance? Pet? Legal?
- What domestic-partner policies will have the biggest impact on my decision? Do I need domestic-partner coverage, regardless of sex?
- Will I need maternal/paternal/parental benefits? Now? In the future?
- What if I only want to work part-time or on a contractual basis? Will I still have the chance to obtain coverage?
- What health benefits do I need beyond insurance? What about wellness programs? Nutritional guidance? Gym membership?
- What financial benefits are most important to me? Retirement? Savings? Investment?
- What am I looking for in terms of vacation? How much? How often? When will there be a raise in days allowed? Will my vacation days carry over? What about holidays? Sick days? Maternity leave? Sabbaticals?
- What childcare options will I need? Is there occasional childcare available in case of emergency?
- What about elder care or other dependent care?
- Could I use pet care? Can I bring my dog to work?
- What side benefits or perks are available to me in this job? Discounts? Logo stuff? Box seats? Tickets? Reward programs? On-site services? Transportation?
- What about education? Can I take classes? Earn degrees while I work? Will my employer help pay or pay in full?
- Are there benefits I know of or would be interested in that haven't been discussed? What might be available? What could I recommend during the interview or after I've been with the company a few months?

1. Esther Wachs Book, "Leadership for the Millennium," *Working Woman* (March 1998): 31.
2. Lynn Densford, "At CIGNA, education is a much-valued benefit," *Corporate University Review* (May–June 1998): 13–19.

# BENEFITS 107

## NOTES

Were there any questions in the benefits checklist that stood out to you? Were there any sections in the benefits chapter that struck you as particularly important or especially relevant to your search? Was there something you feel you should jot down now for later reference? Use this space to record your impressions, your ideas, your wants, and your needs in regard to the sorts of benefits you'll be looking for.

# 9

# Compensation

Finally, we arrive at money. Cold, hard cash. You've been waiting for this chapter, right? From the time we're in elementary school we're taught that we have to get good jobs so we can provide for ourselves and our families, and, in that environment, "good jobs" means "good money." Think about the stack of bills that comes to your mailbox once a month or more often, the rent or the mortgage, the cost of a simple meal or even a not-so-simple meal. Our lives are tied inexorably to money. There can be no doubt about this. So we are all in pursuit of "good jobs" that pay "good money."

And yet, it seems like every time we talk to people about why they left their last job, money isn't the first reason. Sometimes—oftentimes, in fact—money had nothing to do with it. Most people are looking for more than just money in their work. Certainly there have been times when you have caught yourself saying, "there's no *way* I'd do that job—for any amount of money." Or, "No amount of money could keep me here." People are looking for satisfaction in all areas of their working life, from corporate culture, to their relationship with coworkers and leaders, to a feeling of worth and success, and, yes, to the amount of money they make. Money is indeed important. But it is not necessarily the most important thing. Other factors are always involved in job satisfaction.

For those reasons, we've waited until now to include a chapter about compensation. You should include all other aspects of job choice and job satisfaction along with the money issue. Consider not just how much money you want or need, but focus on everything else that you want or need from your next job. In fact, we suggest that in your process of selecting your next job, you leave the money issue fairly low on your list—if you find an opportunity that fulfills your other wants, it's likely that compensation will be more than adequate for your needs. Your new company, if it is an Employer of Choice$^{SM}$—a term we use to define companies that meet and exceed the sorts of criteria we've discussed in this book—is sure to be quite fair in regard to compensation.

That said, we do acknowledge that money is an important factor in your job search, and we'll use this chapter to help you decide how much pay you will need, and to guide you through some of the compensation options that are available to you today.

## Penny-Pinching

*How much money do you have to make?* We'll get to the "want" aspect of this question in a moment, but the "need" issue is slightly more important. The amount of money you must make is the amount of money you need to survive—not just scraping by, but an amount of money that will give you enough cash to save for emergencies. It is a very good idea to get into the habit of putting aside 10 percent of your income "for a rainy day." Unexpected emergencies seem to occur from time to time in all of our lives. If you're lucky enough to avoid them, use that set-aside money to begin building your "nest egg."

You want to make sure that you will be able to afford a reasonable lifestyle before you accept a new job. People often take new jobs for less pay than their previous jobs, for rea-

# COMPENSATION 111

sons including many of the ones we've discussed in previous chapters. If you are considering a career move like that, it is important that you make sure you can still live on your expected new salary.

## YOUR JOB SEARCH

- In order to determine how much money you *must* make, first you must decide if you want to maintain your current lifestyle. If, for instance, you would be willing to move to a less expensive house or apartment, then the amount of money you *must* make will obviously change. And don't forget to include increases or decreases in commuting costs and clothing in your considerations, too.
- Once you have made your lifestyle decision, you should then draw up a budget accordingly. Be sure to include all of your monthly expenses. A sample worksheet that will indicate how much money you must make per month is on the next page. The worksheet is, of course, only provided to assist you in your budgeting process. We hesitate to provide any "hard and fast" rules about your budget.

## A Penny Saved

The 10 percent addition at the bottom of the worksheet is for savings, so that you will not get caught without enough money in an emergency. There is, of course, a difference between how much money you must make and how much money you would like to make.

## Desired Income

*How much money do you want to make?* Whether you are considering future financial goals or immediate ones, this question is an important one. You should still use the following worksheet to determine a starting point, but you can then

# MAKE A COPY OF THIS WORKSHEET—
# YOU MAY WANT TO USE IT MORE THAN ONCE.

## BUDGET WORKSHEET

Rent/Mortgage: .................................. _____

Utilities (phone, electric, gas, cable, etc.): ... _____

Car Payment: ..................................... _____

Auto Insurance: .................................. _____

Credit Cards:  _____                         _____

              _____                          _____

              _____                          _____

Childcare: ....................................... _____

Medical: ......................................... _____

Other: ........................................... _____
    Tuition: ..................................... _____
    Loans: ....................................... _____
    Other Bills: _____                       _____

               _____                       _____

               _____                       _____

Food Costs/month: ............................... _____

Clothing (including dry cleaning): ............. _____

Travel (gas/fare): ............................... _____

Entertainment: ................................... _____

Incidentals (pets, personal, etc.): ............. _____

**TOTAL:**                                        _____

Add 10% (savings):                                _____

**I MUST EARN A NET INCOME OF:**                  _____

factor in other spending decisions that are more closely tied to luxuries, as opposed to necessities. The real answer to this question varies from person to person and depends upon career, experience, talent, hard work, luck in some cases, and several other factors. You should always set high goals for yourself, but in a negotiable situation you should make sure that you set reasonable goals as well.

Something else you should factor in: Don't forget that in accepting a new job, you are not simply considering *present* income, but *future* income as well.

## Getting a Raise

*How soon might you expect a raise?* If moving up the pay scale quickly is important to you, you should consider opportunity for advancement in your search and your decision. Ask about pay scales and structures during the interview process or even during the research process. Employers should be willing and able to discuss opportunities for advancement both in position and salary.

## Competitive Pay

*Have you investigated how competitive the pay is?* We tend to base much of our value as workers on how much money we're paid for doing our job. The dollar amounts have been used as a benchmark for generations, and the practice continues today. While, of course, money is not really an adequate measure of our value or worth, it can go a long way towards helping us feel satisfied about what we do each and every day.

The first consideration in your search should be that you be offered what your market value is. All else being equal, you will of course take the job offered to you that pays more, though as we've discussed, all else is not usually equal. However, you should not accept a job that pays you less than your market worth, unless there are nonmonetary tradeoffs that are more important to you. This idea of worth does not *necessarily* mean that you must see all of your pay in dollars. Remember that we can quite easily assign a dollar value to nonpay-related benefits, and you should look at the entire compensation package *before* coming to a decision.

Pay should also be comparable to the income levels in the community where the employer is located. Pay scales in Boston, for instance, where the cost of living is quite high, should be greater than the pay scales in, say, Albany, Georgia, where the cost of living may be significantly lower. If you are moving, look not necessarily at the dollar amounts, but what those dollars will buy you in your new town.

### REAL-WORLD PRACTICES

When Joyce moved from Westchester County, New York, to Greensboro, North Carolina, in 1996, she was pleased to discover that most of the insurance and taxes she had been accustomed to paying up north were *one-third* as much in her new location.

### HOT TIP

Conduct some research to learn about competitive pay rates in your area. Governmental agencies, chambers of commerce, trade groups, and other organizations conduct studies on a regular basis and can make information available to you. Determine where in the pay scale you think you should fall, then conduct your job search accordingly.

# COMPENSATION

## Overtime

*What sorts of overtime payment options are important to you?* Payment for extra hours varies depending on what sort of job you have—salaried or hourly—and also changes based on what is expected of workers in that field. Hourly jobs almost always have separate overtime rates; you should look closely at (a) what these rates are, and (b) how many hours of overtime may be expected of you. Many hourly pay scales also have rate changes depending on the hours worked, days worked, and number of overtime hours worked.

Compensation for extra time in salaried or contractual positions can be quite a bit more vague. Often, new workers are expected to work long hours, though that trend is changing (see the chapters on culture and benefits) as the power dynamic shifts to the workers. You may have the opportunity to receive hourly pay after you have put in your eight hours, or you may be rewarded later on with promotions or bonuses. Ask about the hours in a typical workday before you agree to specific compensation.

## Bonuses

*What bonus options are important in your decision?* Several kinds of bonus packages and options exist in today's market for workers who go above and beyond the call of duty. We'll detail a few here, but, as always, be sure you ask so that you have all the information needed to make your choice.

- **Year-end:** The most traditional of the bonus/rewards, year-end bonuses are sometimes referred to as "Christmas bonuses." Companies often reward employees with a standard bonus or a percentage bonus of the employee's salary if the company has met or exceeded expectations.

- **Company-based performance:** If the company has done exceedingly well, it may reward all employees or those directly responsible for the success.

- **Employee-based performance:** The company may reward an individual or a group of individuals following the outstanding completion of a project or the accomplishment of a goal. These may be publicized or not, depending upon the situation and the corporate culture.

- **Contractor:** If a contractor has signed on for a specific price but then exceeds expectations, a company may well reward him or her with payment beyond the agreed-upon price.

- **Signing:** Once the domain of sports teams, many companies now offer signing bonuses to new employees. This bonus may, of course, make a significant impact upon your decision regarding not only compensation, but also employment on the whole.

- **Tenure-based:** Companies may reward workers based on their longevity with the organization. This bonus plan should be made known to you during the interview process and in company literature, as, perhaps, should other bonus structures.

## Other Payment Choices

*What other payment options interest you?* Other types of compensation packages beyond hourly and salaried payment do exist, and not simply in the old forms of commissions. Pay scales may change depending upon individual and company performance, and they may move through quite a few levels, depending upon the attainment of a wide variety of targets and goals. These types of payment structures may be negotiated once the job has been offered, or they may be part and parcel of the position. This type of payment is not unlike the incentives built into athletes' contracts. Some of the types of performance-based pay are outlined next.

- **Commissions:** Commissions are based generally upon sales achievement, and a worker is usually paid either a specific dollar amount per sale or a percentage of each sale.

- **Profit-related pay:** Higher compensation goes to workers who more directly affect the success of the company when it succeeds, and belts are tightened when business is not booming. This type of compensation can be part of a salary/bonus combination, as can all of these options.

- **Stock options:** Many public companies offer stock options to employees, sometimes at reduced or frozen prices. Participating employees then benefit all the more when they do their jobs well and the company succeeds. Look into the actual value of these options before you agree to this type of compensation, however; some options can be worth quite a lot of money.

- **Equity:** In some private as well as in some public companies (though in public companies this equity would translate to stock), employees can gain actual equity in the firm itself. In this way, as the value of the company increases, so will the employee's financial worth. By contrast, if the value of the company decreases, so will the financial worth of the employee. So, beware this choice: though it can be quite lucrative, it is of course a double-edged sword.

- **Profit sharing:** Whether in direct payment or payment into retirement plans, profit sharing has become both a buzzword and a desirable part of the overall compensation package. As employees succeed and the company grows, the employees themselves are direct beneficiaries. This type of pay can contribute to your overall satisfaction not simply financially, but in terms of enjoying your job and the camaraderie this type of compensation produces. It's a reward that's tied to your performance.

## REAL-WORLD PRACTICES

Starbucks, the Seattle-based coffee retailer, offers all employees "bean stock." The company wanted to find a way to link shareholder value with long-term rewards for employees, a benefit almost unheard of in privately held companies.

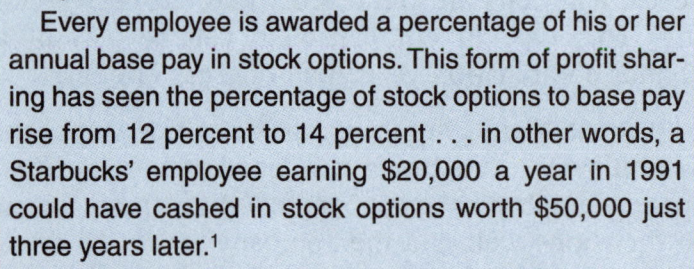

Every employee is awarded a percentage of his or her annual base pay in stock options. This form of profit sharing has seen the percentage of stock options to base pay rise from 12 percent to 14 percent . . . in other words, a Starbucks' employee earning $20,000 a year in 1991 could have cashed in stock options worth $50,000 just three years later.[1]

## YOUR JOB SEARCH

- Whatever compensation package you choose, make sure before you agree to anything that you have contingency plans in place. In other words, if you agree to a performance-based compensation package in whole or even in part, be sure that you will indeed make enough money to maintain your desired standard of living, *even if the company does not perform quite as you or it had hoped.*

## REAL-WORLD PRACTICES

The Edelman Group, a marketing communications firm in New York, has a profit-sharing plan that really makes employees stick around. Terri Edelman, owner, uses a simple plan that is funded entirely by the company. Each year she reviews the firm's finances with her accountant and determines what the contribution to employees will be. During the past ten years, the company has had sales of about $2 million and distributed $500,000.[2]

# COMPENSATION

## Making It Worth Your While

*Is the money you're being offered worth the work?* A simple, easy question, to be sure, but make *sure* the answer is yes. If you feel like you're being paid less than what you're worth or less than what the job is worth, you're going to have an uphill climb to find any sort of job satisfaction at all.

## SUMMARY

We really believe that while compensation is extremely important—after all, you must have money to live—it's not the most important factor in your job search. There are some things you simply wouldn't want to do—no matter what the pay was. However, money is absolutely an important aspect in overall job satisfaction. Look for creative and unique compensation opportunities; don't feel like you have to accept the same old thing. Look for new and different ways to supplement your pay.

Finally: Seek out all of the criteria discussed in this book, and not simply "a lot of money," and we guarantee you'll be happier.

## ASK YOURSELF:
### Choosing a Compensation Package

- How much money *must* I make?
- How much money would I *like* to make?
- What is a realistic combination of the above questions for me?
- How soon will I be able to receive a raise? What are the pay scales like as I move up the ladder? How often do promotions come?
- Will pay increase as my responsibility increases?
- How competitive is the financial package I'm being offered? Are there benefits that provide savings which might offset a lower salary or pay? What really matters to me?

- What sorts of overtime payment options are there?
- Will I be eligible for bonuses? What sorts of bonuses does the company offer?
- Is it possible for me to receive equity? Profit sharing?
- Must I accept salary or hourly pay? May I instead work on commission? On a contract basis?
- What kinds of savings and retirement fund options are available?
- Is the pay I'm being offered worth it?

1. "Starbucks: Making Values Pay," *Fortune* (September 29, 1997): 261–272.
2. Patricia M. Carey, "Just Desserts," *Working Woman* (December/January 1999): 72.

# COMPENSATION

**NOTES**

Were there any questions in the compensation checklist that stood out to you? Were there any sections in the compensation chapter that struck you as particularly important or especially relevant to your search? Was there something you feel you should jot down now for later reference? Use this space to record your impressions, your ideas, your wants, and your needs in regard to the sort of compensation you'll be looking for.

# 10

# The Intangibles

That voice. You've heard it. You've heard it since your very first job in high school. You know the voice. It's familiar. You hear it all the time. You hear it now, or else you wouldn't be reading this book. It's the voice that says, "I don't think I like my job." It's the voice that says, "Something doesn't feel right here." Or, "My job doesn't *mean* anything." "We don't make anything or do anything that matters." "I'm wasting my time." "My life is just passing by, while I sit at this desk . . . in this office . . . at this machine . . . in this truck. . . ." You know the voice.

You bought this book—no, you picked this book up in the first place—because you're hearing the voice. The purpose of this book is to help you eliminate that voice. Using the methods in this book, you'll find greater job satisfaction and be happier in your work and in your life. We've covered what sort of company you should be looking for, how to figure out what industry is right for you, what new and better corporate cultures are emerging in the modern workforce and where to find them, what you can and should expect from your leaders and coworkers, what's going on today in terms of changes in the actual workplace environment, the benefits you should be looking for, and the various means of compensation available to you. We're not quite finished, though.

It's possible that you could find everything you're looking for—it's possible that you thought you had in the past, maybe even in your current job. But something could still be missing. That something is the opportunity for meaningful work; it is the opportunity to feel like you're doing your part to make the world a better place.

Employers of Choice[SM]—the kind of employers who offer the sorts of changes and benefits we've discussed throughout the course of this book—will give you the chance to pursue this idea of meaningful work. Whether you are looking to become the CEO of a multinational corporation or you're looking for an entry-level manufacturing position, meaningful work should be—and is—yours for the asking. You don't have to change the world to find the kind of satisfaction we're talking about. In fact, you don't have to change the world at all. But to complete your process of making the choice, you need to seek out a company that will give you, at the least, the chance on a daily basis to make your small corner of the universe a little bit better place to live—for you and the people who come into contact with you.

In addition to the idea of finding meaningful work, we'll cover some of the other intangibles, some of the other little things that don't necessarily fit easily into categories, but things that you *must* consider before making your choice.

## Making a Difference

*Are you looking for opportunities to make a positive difference?* Almost every organization in any industry is involved in some sort of work that makes a positive difference in the world. Sometimes the benefit to others is direct and obvious; sometimes the benefit is less tangible, less obvious to the world at large, but helps another organization in their drive to make a difference.

One could argue, therefore, that every position in every company has someone, in some way, making a positive difference! If that is so, however, then why do we hear the voice? No, this isn't a trick question. The answer here is simply that some employers are far more diligent and far more successful in both helping their employees see the direct results of the difference they make and in providing opportunities for employees to make a more direct contribution to the company's goals.

You should seek out employers and positions where you can see for yourself the opportunities you'll have to see the results of your work and to help do your part to improve the company, the community, and, in some cases, the world at large.

### Seeing the Results of Your Work

*How can you find companies that allow you to see the results of your work?* One word: ask. Ask your contact, your interviewer, and the person who answers the phone. Ask anyone who will give you an answer how the company works to help its employees see the end results of the jobs they do.

### HOT TIP

Andrew and Roger both worked in landscaping in high school and college because they could see the results of their work right away. "When I was finished," Andrew says, "I could look back at a yard and actually see and look at what I had done. I felt like I'd actually done work." Roger says, "I could measure my results and see my accomplishments."

We're not suggesting that you go right out and buy a lawn mower. We're not asking you to avoid the landscaping industry, either. Just make sure that you're taking a job in which you'll be

*continued*

able to look back at the end of the day or week or year and say, "I can see what I've done." Feeling like you've done good work, meaningful work, work that you can see and feel and be proud of, can be the difference between really finding satisfaction in your job and starting the search process all over again. And don't think you can't find this kind of work in jobs where you don't wear boots and a ball cap, either—plenty of teachers and bankers and real estate managers and the like have jobs with tangible rewards, too.

### REAL-WORLD PRACTICES

At the Volvo Heavy Truck manufacturing plants in Orrville, Ohio, William P. "Phil" Mayes was general manager in the 1980s. Realizing that his stamping plant employees didn't really appreciate the end result of their work, Phil brought a finished Class 8 semi-tractor into the stamping plant. Each employee was able to see how the part he was working on fit on the truck. They developed a sense of pride, like their name was on each piece. Phil used the fresh-off-the-assembly-line truck to take randomly selected employees to lunch at a local restaurant each month. Workers got to ride in a truck they helped build.

## Being Challenged

*Do you want to be challenged?* Of course you do! All of us are looking for jobs in which we have to think, to work to find solutions, to use our capabilities to their maximum potential. The real question is, how can we find these sorts of jobs?

Here's the key: Look for work that you feel will be intellectually stimulating, whether because of variety of tasks needed for a given position, the number of different people with whom you will come into contact during the day, creativity needed to accomplish goals, or any other reason.

# THE INTANGIBLES

Don't take "easy" jobs. It might feel cushy for a while, but you'll end up bored eventually. When you're bored, you're just not going to be happy.

## Finding the Right Job

*How can you find jobs that will be rewarding and challenging?* One way to find these sorts of jobs is through asking questions about working styles. We've discussed these issues in both the leadership and culture chapters of this book, but we'll hit the highlights again here.

A major component in job satisfaction will be how work actually gets done. Companies that encourage collaboration, reward ingenuity and new ideas, and provide nontraditional working spaces to help their people "think outside the box" are a good place to start. You'll learn a lot just by talking to people on the phone, but you can also get a good idea of how things work in the office by just looking around when you're there.

> **HOT TIP**
>
> If you're lucky, you'll be visiting a company on a busy day, on a day when things are really moving. You'll get to see firsthand how the company operates on a tight schedule and in hectic situations. Even if things aren't busy, you'll still be able to get a feel for how the working environment functions, and you'll be able to see how you might fit in.

## Getting on the Same Page

*How can you help potential employers to be as clear as they can be about their expectations of you?* We can't even count the number of times people have told us that they had to leave their jobs because the job itself didn't turn out to be what they thought it would be. Make sure that the employer is clear on what he or she is asking of you, and make sure you are as clear as possible about your understanding of those expectations. Don't get caught in a situation where miscommunication might result in your being unhappy in your new job.

### YOUR JOB SEARCH

- Take notes when you call to inquire about the position, and take notes during your interview.
- At some point in the process, state in your own words what you understand the job requirements to be. That way, if there's been a misunderstanding, you and your interviewer can clear things up right away.

## Making It Yours

*Do you want and/or need ownership of your work?* At many Employers of Choice[SM], responsibility is being pushed lower and lower down the ladder. Employers find that this stimulates hard work and positive results, and employees report greater job satisfaction overall, since the work that they are doing really belongs to them. If this criteria is important to you, find out about how much direct responsibility you would have in the position you are considering, and how much might be available to you as you work your way up through the ranks.

## Feeling Valued

*Do you want to work for a company where you are truly appreciated?* Sometimes appreciation just means a pat on the

# THE INTANGIBLES

back and someone telling you that you did a good job. Sometimes, though, it means much more. As you move through the process, seek out employee-centered work environments. You'll get a good feel for how each company operates as you gain interviewing and exploration experience during your job search. Just keep asking those questions.

> **REAL-WORLD PRACTICES**
>
> The ultimate in demonstrating appreciation for employees came when Malden Mills Industries, Lawrence, Massachusetts, suffered a $300 million fire that destroyed its manufacturing plant. Suddenly, thousands of families were impacted directly and indirectly. In a move that is now legendary, Malden owner Aaron Fuerstein promised to keep all employees on the payroll and rebuild the plant, which makes Polartec fabric. The following year, Malden opened a new $100 million plant on the site of the old building. All but a few of the 1,400 employees returned.[1]

## It's Not Just Numbers

*How can you find companies that are looking at more than just the bottom line?* Business is business, right? Wrong. Businesses are citizens in their communities and of the world just as individuals are, and are therefore beholden to the same ethical responsibilities. You and your company don't have to be changing the world, but you do have the opportunity to be making a difference. Find out about the products and/or services of the companies you are considering. Do they meet ethical standards? Do they hold up to sound moral principles? Is the company doing something out in the world that would make you proud to work for them? Even if the products they make or the services they offer aren't world changing, are the companies using their high position in the community to work for the greater good? If you need the answers to these questions to be "yes," then look for companies that would make you proud to tell your friends and family that you work for them.

> ### REAL-WORLD PRACTICES
> Sometimes the mission isn't about profits at all. An increasing number of companies and their people are working for deeper reasons. More than 40 years ago, a purpose-driven leader named Earl Bakken formed a company called Medtronic, a manufacturer of medical products. The mission statement he wrote in 1960, which has not been changed since, declares that the company's purpose is to "restore people to the fullness of life and health." Even though he's retired, Bakken still meets with every new employee (worldwide) and leads three-hour sessions with groups of 15–20 employees where he describes the founding purpose of the company.
> 
> The most meaningful event of the year for Medtronic's employees is the annual holiday party. There, employees hear the personal stories of the patients whose lives have been saved and restored by Medtronic products. Bill George, president and CEO, stresses "leading by values" rather than "management by objectives." Medtronic's stated values (in order) are "restoring people to full health, serving your customers with products and services of unsurpassed quality, recognizing the personal worth of employees, making a fair profit and return for shareholders, and maintaining good citizenship as a company."
> 
> Medtronic employees really have the opportunity to see the good that they are doing in their communities and in the world. They feel good about themselves each day when they go to work, because they know their products are, quite literally, saving people's lives.[2]

# THE INTANGIBLES  131

## Changing the World

*Is the idea of making the world a better place a bit overwhelming to you?* It should be. What a huge idea! Some of the world's most respected thinkers and philosophers have been unable to fully understand this concept. Though we're not eliminating thinking and philosophy as job choices here, we certainly don't expect you to get a clear idea of changing the world in one reading of this book or in a lifetime of study.

You don't have to change the world by yourself. Helping just one organization, working for one cause, or assisting one family or even one person can really make a difference. Finding a company that allows you to pursue even these modest goals can give you an opportunity to make a difference.

> **REAL-WORLD PRACTICES**
>
> Each department of Arizona Mail Order, one of the largest mail-order companies in the country, adopts a needy family from the local community during the December holiday season. The teams from each of the departments hold in-company bake sales and do other things to raise money. Then team members shop together for food and gifts for their family. On Christmas Eve, the members of the department, as a group, deliver the goodies to the needy family.

There are a number of worthwhile alternatives within the umbrella of corporate citizenship. At the local level, there are opportunities for companies to participate in economic development, literacy development programs, downtown fix-up, kids programs, activities for the elderly, cultural events, and much, much more. Chambers of Commerce provide leadership, and so do Rotary Clubs, Kiwanis, and other worthwhile organizations.

Beyond the local level, there are regional and national opportunities for involvement. Save the Children, United Way, American Red Cross, and Boy and Girl Scouts of America are just a few of the service organizations with which you can become involved through your company. Individuals and companies can also provide assistance for victims of floods, hurricanes, and other disasters. On a global level, corporations support programs to feed the hungry and efforts to stop the exploitation of children. Foundations, international relief organizations, religious groups, and a wide range of civic and professional organizations help facilitate personal and corporate support for those in need.

## YOUR JOB SEARCH

- Is there a specific cause or charity that is crucially important in your life? One with which you are already deeply involved? If corporate citizenship is one of those "make-it-or-break-it" issues in your job search, contact the nonprofit organization(s) involved and obtain a list of *its* corporate supporters. You can then see if there might be opportunities within those corporations before expanding your job search.

### REAL-WORLD PRACTICES

Burrell Professional Labs, the world's largest network of portrait and wedding photographic labs, has long been considered the nation's premiere photo finisher for professional photographers. Don Burrell, president, believes in sharing the wealth his company earns. To mark his 40th year in business, he pledged $40,000 to the Professional Photographers Association Charities. The 1999 beneficiary was the Elizabeth Glaser Pediatric AIDS Foundation. Don founded the Burrell Cancer Institute at the St. Anthony Medical Center in the company's hometown of Crown Point, Indiana. He and his employees also supported construction of a 30-bed shelter for battered women and their children.

# THE INTANGIBLES

## Volunteering

*Are you looking for specific volunteer opportunities connected to your next job?* As corporations look for greater and greater exposure (and, on a less cynical note, opportunities to give back to their communities), they provide increasing opportunities for employees to volunteer for local charities or civic groups. Find out about such opportunities at any employer you are considering.

### REAL-WORLD PRACTICES

Brink's Home Security gives one day off per year to every employee to volunteer in community service. Timberland employees may use up to 40 hours of paid time per year for volunteer work. Other companies encourage employees to volunteer four hours a week and allow flexibility in working hours to accommodate people attending meetings or providing direct services in civic organizations.

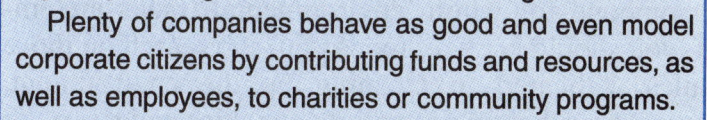

Plenty of companies behave as good and even model corporate citizens by contributing funds and resources, as well as employees, to charities or community programs.

### REAL-WORLD PRACTICES

HA-LO Industries, a Chicago-based specialty advertising firm, is known for its charitable work. Each year, the company sends hundreds of underprivileged children to professional sporting events. The HA-LO Kids Heaven program has provided free tickets to Chicago Bulls and Chicago White Sox games for years. Over 2000 deserving kids benefit from this program each year, attending games with employees of HA-LO right there with them.

## Better Ways to Sleep at Night

*What else can you do to find rewarding opportunities in your next job?* Many companies participate in smaller projects in an effort to help their communities, and to give their employees opportunities to contribute to the ongoing process of finding meaningful work and meaningful roles in their lives.

- **Fund-raising:** Walkathons, bikeathons, and even rockathons are great vehicles for raising money for charity without demanding large or ongoing time commitments from already busy employees. Many organizations provide opportunities for employees to give in this way, without demanding even more from their increasingly hectic schedules. Almost everyone can find one night or one weekend to help other people.

- **Highway cleanups and other greenspace possibilities:** Have you seen the Adopt-a-Highway signs where you live? If you're an avid environmentalist, or just someone who'd like to keep things a little cleaner, look for companies committed to cleanups of various kinds in and around their communities. It goes without saying, though, that if you're someone for whom environmental issues are important, you should actively focus your job search on those companies dedicated to cleaning up the environment, those companies that do not pollute our skies and rivers, or those companies that have products and services that are either environmentally friendly or environmentally inert.

- **Helping kids:** Companies adopt schools, classes, or even special groups of students. Some offer tutoring services, mentoring programs, or scholarships. You can get involved one-on-one through programs like Junior Achievement or Kids-at-Work days.

- **Community assistance:** Community cleanups and service projects are just the tip of the iceberg in terms of how you can get involved on the local level. Habitat for Humanity actively solicits corporate support—financial and hands-on labor—and other charities and civic groups need help,

# THE INTANGIBLES 135

too. Companies provide volunteers at senior citizens homes, for youth organizations such as scouting and 4-H, and for a variety of other civic needs.

- **Emergency response:** All you need to do is to flip on the evening news to see natural disasters affecting communities across the country. God forbid a disaster should strike your town, but if it does, your company may be in a position to help those who need it. There may be nothing more rewarding than coming to the aid of someone desperately in need of the assistance.

### REAL-WORLD PRACTICES

Datatel, Inc., a Fairfax, Virginia, developer of software for colleges and universities, is a 350-employee company that has very few people leave for other jobs. An integral part of Datatel's culture is giving back to the community. Every May 1, the company's Founder's Day, employees, family, and friends participate in a community service day. They've remodeled a house, rebuilt trails at a local park, helped with track and field events for Special Olympics, and helped make a child's wish come true through the Make a Wish Foundation. Some employees of this company mentor and tutor students at a local elementary school. Through their Datatel Scholars Foundation, the company has awarded over $1.2 million to over 1000 students who are enrolled at their client sites.

### REAL-WORLD PRACTICES

At Patrice Tanaka & Company, Inc., a public relations firm in New York, each year employees are given Valentine's Day off. They use this time to show their love for their fellow man by performing community service work.

## REAL-WORLD PRACTICES

When Hurricane Floyd caused unprecedented damage and personal loss in North Carolina—mostly from flooding—many corporations sprang to the rescue. Boddie-Noell, an operator of over 350 Hardee's Restaurants and other ventures, is based in Rocky Mount, North Carolina, one of the areas hardest hit by the storm. The company's attention was immediately focused upon their people and their communities. During the initial recovery period, the company arranged for two truckloads of critically needed drinking water to be distributed in their home area of Nash and Edgecombe Counties.

Next, the attention turned to relief efforts. Company restaurants outside the affected area collected food, clothing, and supplies for coworkers and others in the flooded communities. All the stores got involved in fund-raising and produced over $100,000 for flood victims. The company then focused on the 18 employees whose families were displaced by Hurricane Floyd. A home office team member assumed responsibility for follow-through with each family, with care continuing long after the storm was gone. One effort focused on making sure that every child in a displaced family still had a great Christmas. The company's culture was reflected in the corporate and employee response to care for any employee who needed help with an outpouring of love and warmth.

## HOT TIP

Looking for a company oriented towards community service? Check with local branches of charities and civic organizations for donor lists and volunteer activity logs. You can also research companies' civic activity in business databases, or simply through local contacts.

# THE INTANGIBLES 137

## SUMMARY

All else said, discussed, and dissected, sometimes it's the little things—the intangibles—that make the difference in you being satisfied with your new job. Consider what little things you have missed in your previous jobs, and even what sort of intangibles you'd be looking for in a dream job. You never know: you may just find a company that's offering *exactly* what you're looking for. Accounting with a chance to build homes for less fortunate people once a month? Working a factory line assembling a product that will make young mothers' lives immeasurably easier? You never know until you start looking. The opportunities are there.

### ASK YOURSELF: The Intangibles

- Is my work meaningful? How important is finding a deeper meaning in my work?
- Where can I make a positive difference? Will I change the world tomorrow morning? Next week? Next year?
- Do I want to work on a smaller scale to change my community?
- Can I see the results of my work in my present job? How can I make sure I'll be able to in the next one? What is it that I want to do, and what results do I want to see on a daily basis? Each week? In five years?
- Am I being challenged now? What do I need to look for to ensure that I'll be challenged in my next job?
- How can I find rewarding and challenging jobs?
- Do I understand what the job that I am considering entails? How sure am I? Have I made sure the company and I agree on expectations?
- How important is "owning" my work to me? How can I make the work I do mine?
- Am I appreciated—really—in my present job? What will it take for me to feel appreciated in my next job?

- ❏ Do I need a company concerned about more than just productivity and the bottom line? Should the employer be concerned about the community? The environment? The country? The world? What areas of interest are most important to me?
- ❏ What opportunities are available to make my work and my life more meaningful through the employer I am considering?
- ❏ Do I need or want civic volunteer activities at my next place of employment?

## YOUR JOB SEARCH

- Is there something we've missed? Is there something you have to have in order to accept a job offer? A benefit? Some aspect of working conditions? *WRITE IT DOWN.* If it's still on your mind after reading this book, it's obviously important to you. You should treat this factor as important or even more important than any we've discussed. This consideration doesn't mean you should throw the book out the window, but use the information you've gathered and the things you've learned about yourself and your needs to guide your search. Simply add whatever criteria we've missed, one that is specific to you or to your situation, to the list of criteria you're looking for in your next job. It's that easy.

### Add your extra criteria here:

_____

_____

_____

---

1. Rhonda K. Miller, "Workers to Be Paid While Company Rebuilds," *Human Resource Executive.* (April 1999): 42.
2. "Work Rich with Purpose and Meaning," *At Work* (October 1993): 13.

# THE INTANGIBLES 139

## NOTES
Were there any questions in the intangibles checklist that stood out to you? Were there any sections in the intangibles chapter that struck you as particularly important or especially relevant to your search? Was there something you feel you should jot down now for later reference? Use this space to record your impressions, your ideas, your wants, and your needs in regard to the sorts of intangibles you'll be looking for.

# Part Three
# Conclusion

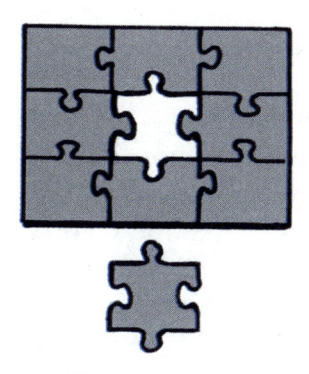

# 11

# Putting It All Together

Well, you're finished. You've read the book and now you know everything there is to know about your job search. Right?

Of course not. There is no one book that can tell you *everything* you need to know about your job search. Keep in mind that the most important tool in all of this is the one that you keep up on top of your shoulders and neck. Only you will know, in the end, what's best for you.

## An Overview of a Different Color

Our intention here is to provide a tool, a map of sorts, to help you in this very difficult, very important, and often very complicated process. We know firsthand the fear and exhilaration of the prospect of changing jobs—we've both done it many times! What this book can do—and by now has done—is to give you actual ink-on-paper information about the kinds of things you should be looking for in your next job. By now you've gone through the introduction, made copies of the appendices and read the seven main chapters about the sorts of things you can expect in your job search. We hope you've read about a few things you didn't know you could expect. Did you know before you read this book that some companies will let you take your dog to work with you? Will insure against bad weather on your vacation? Will pay you bonuses for recruiting your friends to join you at work? Will support your volunteer efforts?

Apply your thinking to determine the kinds of criteria you want to use in your job search. Follow the directions on the scoresheets and use all of the worksheets. In fact: no dessert for you until you've done all your work! Seriously, though, make the most of the time and energy you've invested in reading these pages and making decisions—some of them easy, quick choices, and some of them difficult. Pay attention to each kind of choice, and listen to your heart, your head, and, most especially, your gut, as you go along.

The market has changed out there—*in a fundamental way*. Unemployment rates are dropping, the economy is expanding in some places, booming in others . . . *the competitive advantage has shifted*. The way employment decisions are made and job searches are conducted must change to keep up with the times. The advantage no longer rests solely with the employer. You now have a lot of power and influence as you conduct your job search. You have choices.

In your parents' generation—even in your own, a mere five or ten years ago—the way a job search and employment would go was this: you'd read the want ads, send out a stack of letters and resumes, wait patiently by the mailbox, interview for a few positions, and then make sacrifices to the gods of employment and bank accounts. You'd rejoice at the prospect of even one offer, much less two, and take *whatever* they were offering . . . and be happy to have it. Then you'd work traditional nine-to-five hours, or much longer hours, or happily take third shift . . . and you'd do the same thing for *years*. After a while, you'd get up on a Tuesday morning, brush your teeth with muscle-ache cream and rub your aching neck with smooth-mint gel toothpaste, stare into the mirror, and think, "I can't go to work today." Or, "I wonder if I can call in sick. Did I do that last week?" Or, "My job is sucking the life right out of me. If I have to sit in one more meeting with Bob from accounting, I'm going to light everyone's desk on fire."

But now . . .

## Why It's OK to Joke About This

Because it's fun! Why should we not be able to laugh at ourselves about these things? "We" can mean anyone you'd like—your former bosses, the authors of this book, your current coworkers, you and your friends at dinner on a Saturday night. "We" should be able to have *fun* at work. "We" should be able to enjoy talking *about* work.

Employment doesn't have to be like it's always been, and, in fact, in today's market, it isn't. Employers see the competitive advantage shifting, too, just as workers do, and they're taking steps to make their employment opportunities better, more rewarding, and more challenging. Just as you are in search of the perfect job for you, they're in search of the perfect worker for them.

What you are seeking—and what the employers out there are seeking—is a mutually beneficial relationship. You'll be happier in a job you like, and they'll be happier with a satisfied worker, because the work you do will be more valuable *both to you and to them*. It's a win-win situation.

Not every job out there is great and perfect. Not every employee at every employer is forever engaged in a struggle not to break into song at any moment of the day because of how happy they are in their jobs. Some employers are still behind the times. Some employees have jobs that are just a bad fit.

Some people are at the wrong company or in the wrong career altogether.

In fact, that's why you have this book in your hands right now. It's the voice we talked about in the "Intangibles" chapter. Something in there is nagging at you, telling you there's something missing in your current job. Something's not right. You're not having *fun*.

It's not such a crazy notion, you know, that your work should be fun. After all, why not? Why shouldn't we look for jobs that are rewarding and that we feel good about and that are actually fun? Who doesn't want to be able to come home at the end of the day and think, "Today, I made a difference. Today, my job meant something. Today, I enjoyed my work."

Who doesn't want to get up on those Tuesday mornings and look into the mirror while brushing their teeth with the correct product, and look forward to the activities of the day?

## Nuts and Bolts

*Wait—No Resume Sending, No Waiting for Job Offers. . . What, Then?* Actually, many of the same processes from the way job searches worked in the past will still be in place for years to come. Even if you find a posting on the Web instead of in the paper, you'll still need to inquire about an opening, send a resume, or fill out an application, and you'll still need to go through the interview process and wait for an offer.

However, in this market, it's likely that the offers you do receive will be greater in number and in opportunity. And when you do receive those offers or interviews, you'll have the chance to ask some of the questions as well. You should let the hiring authority know right away that you're looking for an opportunity that will be a mutually beneficial match for you *and* the company, an opportunity for you to find value in and enjoy your work, and an opportunity for them to get the most out of you and your abilities.

# PUTTING IT ALL TOGETHER 147

Be careful and cautious in your interview. You don't want to come off as cocky and overconfident. The decision, after all, still rests with them initially. Your decision making process is certainly in gear at the interview stage, but it won't really kick into high gear until after they've made an offer and you must decide whether or not to accept.

In questions, push for the answers you need. Just be sure that you remain professional and polite as you probe for answers to questions about benefits and culture and the like.

## Ultimately, You Are in Charge

This point is really important: *You are ultimately in control of your own career destiny.* We think this point may be the most distinct difference between today's work environment and the markets of years past. Before, workers believed that employers were in control of employees' careers, and, in some instances, they were right. In the current marketplace, though, as workers and tasks become increasingly fluid and the idea of one job for one's entire career becomes a bit antiquated, it is the employees *themselves* who are in charge of mapping their own career paths.

## And Keep in Mind

As you begin your search and follow it through to the interview and offer stages, there are a few things you really must keep in mind. These factors will help you determine the relative importance of the work you've done as you moved through this book. These factors will also help you narrow your search and eventually make a choice.

## YOUR JOB SEARCH

- Mapping your career path: As we've said, you are now in charge of your own career path. As you set about making your choice, think about where you want to be, career-wise, in six months, a year, five years, ten years . . . will the job you're considering help you get there? Will the company? What do you want to be doing right now? Eventually?

- You are no longer mandated to follow a linear career path: It used to be all about moving steadily up the ladder, until you were the assistant vice assistant to the president's assistant . . . until you had some sort of fancy title on your business cards . . . until you had business cards. These days, though, people are increasingly following "hopscotch" career paths. Hopscotch career paths don't have to go in straight lines; they remove the stigma of making lateral career moves *or even backward career moves*. Remember: moving backwards is OK, too! If you need to take a step back to put yourself on the right track to be doing what you really want to do, then do it!

- Put your life balance ahead of your career management: "Get a life," so to speak. More importantly, keep the one you've built or the one you're building. Your life—your spouse, girlfriend, boyfriend, dog, goldfish, Frisbee, buddies, family—is going to be, and should be, more important than your job. Your work does not necessarily have to define you. Some of us are lucky enough to find a synthesis of life and work, but for those of us whose lives are separate from our work, it is important that we remember to place a premium on the work/life balance we need. It won't always be about the money or the career advancement—the decision might be largely affected by how much time you get to spend at home, living your life.

- It's OK to always be looking for your next job: Employers don't necessarily believe you're going to spend the rest of your life with them

# PUTTING IT ALL TOGETHER 149

any more than you do. It's OK to look at a potential job in terms of the skills you will learn that will be applicable in your next job. It's OK to be looking for skills and experiences to add to your "bag of tricks," to add to your resume. It's OK to be looking ahead to how this job will make you more marketable in the future. After all, as the workforce changes and becomes much more fluid—people will jump from job to job about every two to four years—it seems not only reasonable, but expected, that you should always be looking ahead. You may not move so frequently, but the societal trend is in place. Workers are restless and will continue searching.

- It may be OK to tell your employer how long you're planning to stay: No, we're not crazy. This conversation can be very tricky, and we recommend that you be careful here. But it's not unreasonable to discuss how long you're planning to stay when interviewing for a job. There is, indeed, the possibility of discussing and even setting your departure date. This discussion will give the company the best chance to get the most out of you, and to either look for your replacement as the time comes or to look for ways to entice you to stay. Have in mind what sort of commitment you'll be willing to make to your employer as you move through the search process.
- It's OK to look for fun work: It is, really. There is so much available to you, so many opportunities are out there, that you can afford to look for fun, meaningful work. That, in essence, is what the job search is all about: moving between jobs and companies until you find the right fit, the right job, the right people . . . the right work for you. Keep looking until you find that right job. Remember that as you move down the career path your needs will change, and what is right for you today may not be right for you ten years down the road.

## One More Thing

There is only one more thing we have to add: *When you do find the right place and the right fit, **stay there***. That's what the whole thing is about after all. You're looking for fun work, for job satisfaction, for happiness in your career and in your life. We all know how dissatisfaction at work can spread into other aspects of your life. So, when you do find the right fit, put this book down for a while. Find a good spot on your shelf so that you can find it again, if you need it. Stay at that job for as long as you can, for as long as you want. Enjoy the environment and benefits you sought.

You have a great freedom in this economy. You can be happy in your job. You can have fun at work. You can find meaningful and satisfying employment. Pick up those worksheets and scoresheets again. You have what you need to find that elusive perfect job right in front of you. Get to it—and good luck!

# Appendix A

## Scoresheets

*In the box next to each statement, place a ranking from -5 to +5 depending on how important each statement is to you in your job search. Each scoresheet corresponds to a chapter in Part II.*

### The Company

[   ] I want to work for a market leader.
[   ] I want to work for a company with excellent name recognition.
[   ] I want to work for a company with a high market share.
[   ] I want to work for a company with excellent profit margins.
[   ] I want to work for a large company.
[   ] I want to work for a small company.
[   ] I want to work for a start-up.
[   ] I want to work for a company on the leading edge.
[   ] I want to use my current skills in my next job.
[   ] The company must accommodate my current career goals.
[   ] The company must accommodate my future career goals.
[   ] I can join a company that is at greater risk at this point in my career.

[ ] I need to join a company that is financially secure.
[ ] The history of the company is important to me.
[ ] Stability in terms of market position is important to me.
[ ] I want to work for a company with a low incidence of employee turnover.
[ ] I want to have a clear idea of the company's past.
[ ] I want to have a clear idea of where the company is headed.
[ ] I want to know about current products and services.
[ ] I want to know what future products and services are in development.
[ ] I need to know who the company's clients are.
[ ] I need the employer to be well known in the industry.
[ ] My next employer should be highly regarded in its industry.
[ ] I need the employer to be highly regarded in the community.
[ ] The quality of goods and services is an important factor in my decision.
[ ] The inherent social value of the company's goods and services is an important factor in my decision.
[ ] When I think about the company I'm considering, I feel good about working there.

## The Culture

[ ] The way a company "feels" is important to me.
[ ] I need a relaxed atmosphere.
[ ] I need a supercharged atmosphere.
[ ] I need a more traditional workplace.
[ ] I like to work on my own.
[ ] I like to work in groups.
[ ] I like to have my assignments given to me.
[ ] Standards are important to my job satisfaction.
[ ] It's important that the company I work for have a high standard of quality and service.

# SCORESHEETS 153

[ ] Quality of products and service can make the difference in my decision.
[ ] The quality and ability of my coworkers affects my job satisfaction.
[ ] I have a strong need for honesty and ethics.
[ ] I need my employer to place a premium on honesty and ethics.
[ ] Issues of racial equality are crucial to me.
[ ] Issues of gender-based equality are crucial to me.
[ ] Issues of age-based equality are crucial to me.
[ ] Issues of equality based on sexual orientation are crucial to me.
[ ] I need a company that values experience.
[ ] I need a company that hires based on talent alone.
[ ] I need a company that values tenure.
[ ] I want to work for a "young" company.
[ ] I want a chance to have a mentoring relationship in my next job.
[ ] I like to work in a social setting.
[ ] I need to be largely left alone at work.
[ ] I need to find ways to enjoy my job more.
[ ] I need the company to help me find ways to enjoy my job more.
[ ] I want a formal workplace.
[ ] I want an informal workplace.
[ ] I want a casual dress code.
[ ] I want to be on a first-name basis with everyone.
[ ] I want to work in a traditional office layout.
[ ] I want a less traditional office.
[ ] I want to work with the latest technologies.
[ ] I need to feel connected to my coworkers.
[ ] I need to feel connected to my bosses.
[ ] Internal communication is important to me.
[ ] I need for people to listen to my ideas.
[ ] I want to feel company spirit.
[ ] I want to have friends at work.

## Leadership and Working Styles

[ ] I want a laid-back boss.
[ ] I want a coach.
[ ] I want a mentor.
[ ] I want a taskmaster.
[ ] I need to be pushed to get all my work done.
[ ] I want to be left to complete projects in my own ways.
[ ] I want to like my boss.
[ ] I want to respect my boss.
[ ] I want for my boss to respect my opinion.
[ ] I want a much less formal relationship with the people above me.
[ ] I prefer traditional leader/employee relationships.
[ ] I want to feel like my coworkers are happy in their jobs.
[ ] I want my boss to be highly accessible.
[ ] I want to feel like I can ask my leaders anything.
[ ] I want to feel like I can always talk to my boss.
[ ] I want to be able to voice concerns easily and safely.
[ ] I want to be able to offer suggestions about how to do things better.
[ ] I want a lot of responsibility in my next job.
[ ] I don't want a lot of responsibility.
[ ] I want successes to be my responsibility and failures to be my fault.
[ ] I want the company to be open to change.
[ ] Open working environments suit me best.
[ ] I want a more traditional office/cubicle working area.
[ ] I want opportunities for promotion.
[ ] I want opportunities for transfer.
[ ] I need to feel like the company wants me.
[ ] I want the company to have minimal office politics.

## Environment

[ ] Location is important to me.
[ ] I want to work downtown.
[ ] I want to work uptown.

# SCORESHEETS

[ ] I want to work in a rural area.
[ ] I want to work in the suburbs.
[ ] I want to work in _____.
[ ] I need to be out of the office on a regular basis.
[ ] I want to travel.
[ ] I need the workplace to be close to the interstate.
[ ] I need access to public transportation.
[ ] I want to be close to home.
[ ] I want to be able to walk to work.
[ ] I want to be able to bike to work.
[ ] I want employee carpools.
[ ] I would be willing to move or transfer to another office.
[ ] I would be willing to move or relocate to another city or state.
[ ] I need a 9 to 5 schedule.
[ ] I want to work the _____ to _____ shift.
[ ] I want to work _____ hours per week.
[ ] I need/want to work from home some of the time.
[ ] I need/want to work from home all of the time.
[ ] I need/want to telecommute.
[ ] I want a better quality of work life.
[ ] I want to spend no more than _____ hours per week at work.
[ ] I want to spend no fewer than _____ hours per week at home.
[ ] I want to work in an office.
[ ] I can work in cubicles.
[ ] I refuse to work in cubicles.
[ ] I like traditional office layouts.
[ ] I would be interested in an open office.
[ ] I need to be able to personalize my workspace.
[ ] I want to work in teams.
[ ] I want to work alone.
[ ] I want to work directly for someone else.
[ ] I need to be able to get away from the office for breaks.
[ ] I need on-site break areas.
[ ] I need on-site or close-by eating opportunities.

[ ] I want modern facilities and the latest equipment and technology.
[ ] I want to work at a desk.
[ ] I want to work where I'll be around people.
[ ] I want to work on the sales floor.
[ ] I want to work in assembly.
[ ] I want a window.
[ ] I want to work outside.
[ ] I want to work inside.
[ ] I want my job to be different every day.
[ ] I would be willing to wear a uniform.
[ ] I would be willing to wear a suit every day.
[ ] I need a "blue jeans" environment.

## Benefits

[ ] I need basic health insurance.
[ ] I need expanded health insurance.

I want/need the following coverage:

[ ] Dental
[ ] Vision
[ ] Maternal/paternal
[ ] Mental health
[ ] I want/need special insurance options.
[ ] I want creative insurance options, such as pet insurance.
[ ] I want group auto insurance.
[ ] I want group homeowners/renters insurance.
[ ] I need benefits extended to domestic partners.
[ ] I want maternal/paternal leave.
[ ] I want to be able to work part-time or contractually and still have benefits options.
[ ] I want health benefits beyond insurance.
[ ] I need wellness programs.
[ ] I need health club membership options.
[ ] I want retirement programs.
[ ] I want savings programs.

# SCORESHEETS 157

[ ] I want investment programs.
[ ] I want _____ weeks of vacation.
[ ] I must have the ability to take _____ holidays.
[ ] I want my vacation and sick days to carry over.
[ ] I'm looking for _____ sick days.
[ ] I want the opportunity to take sabbaticals.
[ ] I need on-site childcare.
[ ] I need some sort of subsidized childcare.
[ ] I need emergency childcare for snow days and the like.
[ ] I need elder care and/or dependent care options.
[ ] I want creative benefits choices, like the chance to bring my pet to work, or _____.
[ ] I want side benefits like perks, discounts, tickets, reward programs, or _____.
[ ] I want my employer to pay for all or part of my education.
[ ] I want the chance to earn _____ degree while I'm working.
[ ] I need or want the following benefit: _____.

## Compensation

[ ] I must make $ _____ per week/month/year.
[ ] I would like to make $ _____ per week/month/year.
[ ] I think a realistic goal for compensation is $ _____, and I won't take less money than that.
[ ] I want to receive a raise in _____ months.
[ ] The pay of jobs above me is important to me.
[ ] I want to be promoted in _____ months.
[ ] I want pay to increase as my responsibility does.
[ ] I want the financial package to be competitive with industry norms.
[ ] I would be willing to consider items other than money as part of the overall compensation package.
[ ] Overtime payment is important to me.
[ ] Bonus structures are important to me.
[ ] I want a year-end bonus.

- [ ] I want a signing bonus.
- [ ] I want performance-based bonuses.
- [ ] I want to have a regular salary.
- [ ] I prefer to work on commission or a pay-for-performance basis.
- [ ] I want to be able to receive equity in the company.
- [ ] I want profit-sharing options.
- [ ] I want stock options.
- [ ] I want savings and retirement funds.
- [ ] I want to feel like the pay is worth the job. That number is: _____ .

## Intangibles

- [ ] I want my work to be meaningful.
- [ ] I want to find a deeper purpose in my work.
- [ ] I want to make a positive difference in the world.
- [ ] I want to make a positive difference in my community.
- [ ] I want to be able to see the results of my work.
- [ ] I want to be doing what *I* want to do.
- [ ] I want to pursue my dream job.
- [ ] I want to get paid for doing what I love.
- [ ] I've always wanted to _____ .
- [ ] I want to be doing _____ in six months, in a year, in five years, in ten years.
- [ ] I want challenging work.
- [ ] I want difficult work.
- [ ] I want to have to find new solutions every day.
- [ ] My work must be rewarding.
- [ ] I need to have a clear idea of what would be required in the job I'm considering.
- [ ] I want the work I do to be mine.
- [ ] I want credit for my work.
- [ ] I want recognition for a job well done.
- [ ] I want to feel appreciated in my next job.

# SCORESHEETS

[ ] I want a company concerned with giving back to the community.
[ ] I want opportunities to enhance civic life in my next job.
[ ] I want to work for a responsible corporate citizen.
[ ] I want to work for a socially conscious company.
[ ] I want to work for a company that espouses these social and political views: _____.
[ ] I want volunteer opportunities in my next job.
[ ] I want my job to make my life more meaningful.
[ ] I want a better work/life balance.
[ ] I want to love my job.
[ ] I want to have fun.

APPENDIX A

## *WORKSHEET ONE*

List all of the items that you scored a +5. These are the things you really need to focus on in your job search. *Once you have listed these items, work to weave them into a paragraph or two about what you need out of your next job.* In that way, you'll have a more concise idea of what you are looking for. When the time comes to articulate those wants/needs to a potential employer, you'll already have them written down once—so you won't be saying it for the first time. You will also want to list all of your -5 items—those things you really want to avoid in your next job.

**List +5 Items Here**

_____
_____
_____
_____
_____
_____
_____
_____
_____
_____
_____
_____
_____
_____

# WORKSHEETS

## List -5 Items Here

**Use this page to write out the description of your ideal job in words:**

# WORKSHEETS

## WORKSHEET TWO

List all of your +4 and +3 items, and do the same with your -3 and -4 scores. These items will still be important in your job search. Writing them down again will help you keep them fresh in your mind as you begin your search. Items that you have scored between -2 and +2 may still be important, but they will not necessarily be deciding factors in the process.

_____
_____
_____
_____
_____
_____
_____
_____
_____
_____
_____
_____
_____
_____
_____
_____
_____
_____
_____
_____
_____
_____

## WORKSHEET THREE

We've provided several worksheets for you to fill out about your previous jobs to help you evaluate what you liked and disliked about those positions. After all, you are the expert on what works and doesn't work *for you*. If you need more sheets than those that we've provided here, simply make copies as necessary.

Job: _____

My title: _____

My job responsibilities included:
_____
_____
_____
_____

My wages/salary: $ _____ / month / year

The compensation was fair/not fair because:
_____
_____
_____

Things I really liked about the job:
_____
_____
_____

Things I did not like about the job:
_____
_____
_____

# WORKSHEETS

I wish I'd had the chance to:
_____
_____

The people I worked with were:
_____
_____
_____

I would/would not like to find people like that again.

I liked the way(s) my boss . . .
_____
_____
_____

I really did not like the way my boss . . .
_____
_____
_____

Things I want to do in my next job that I did in this job:
_____
_____
_____

Things I'll never do again:
_____
_____
_____
_____

Use your answers here in conjunction with your answers from the scoresheets to help you continue to hone in on exactly what you're looking for.

*No, there's nothing wrong with your book. We've given you a second copy of Appendix A for your subsequent job search(es).*

## The Company

[ ] I want to work for a market leader.
[ ] I want to work for a company with excellent name recognition.
[ ] I want to work for a company with a high market share.
[ ] I want to work for a company with excellent profit margins.
[ ] I want to work for a large company.
[ ] I want to work for a small company.
[ ] I want to work for a start-up.
[ ] I want to work for a company on the leading edge.
[ ] I want to use my current skills in my next job.
[ ] The company must accommodate my current career goals.
[ ] The company must accommodate my future career goals.
[ ] I can join a company that is at greater risk at this point in my career.

[ ] I need to join a company that is financially secure.
[ ] The history of the company is important to me.
[ ] Stability in terms of market position is important to me.
[ ] I want to work for a company with a low incidence of employee turnover.
[ ] I want to have a clear idea of the company's past.
[ ] I want to have a clear idea of where the company is headed.
[ ] I want to know about current products and services.
[ ] I want to know what future products and services are in development.
[ ] I need to know who the company's clients are.
[ ] I need the employer to be well known in the industry.
[ ] My next employer should be highly regarded in its industry.
[ ] I need the employer to be highly regarded in the community.
[ ] The quality of goods and services is an important factor in my decision.
[ ] The inherent social value of the company's goods and services is an important factor in my decision.
[ ] When I think about the company I'm considering, I feel good about working there.

## The Culture

[ ] The way a company "feels" is important to me.
[ ] I need a relaxed atmosphere.
[ ] I need a supercharged atmosphere.
[ ] I need a more traditional workplace.
[ ] I like to work on my own.
[ ] I like to work in groups.
[ ] I like to have my assignments given to me.
[ ] Standards are important to my job satisfaction.
[ ] It's important that the company I work for have a high standard of quality and service.

# SCORESHEETS

[ ] Quality of products and service can make the difference in my decision.
[ ] The quality and ability of my coworkers affects my job satisfaction.
[ ] I have a strong need for honesty and ethics.
[ ] I need my employer to place a premium on honesty and ethics.
[ ] Issues of racial equality are crucial to me.
[ ] Issues of gender-based equality are crucial to me.
[ ] Issues of age-based equality are crucial to me.
[ ] Issues of equality based on sexual orientation are crucial to me.
[ ] I need a company that values experience.
[ ] I need a company that hires based on talent alone.
[ ] I need a company that values tenure.
[ ] I want to work for a "young" company.
[ ] I want a chance to have a mentoring relationship in my next job.
[ ] I like to work in a social setting.
[ ] I need to be largely left alone at work.
[ ] I need to find ways to enjoy my job more.
[ ] I need the company to help me find ways to enjoy my job more.
[ ] I want a formal workplace.
[ ] I want an informal workplace.
[ ] I want a casual dress code.
[ ] I want to be on a first-name basis with everyone.
[ ] I want to work in a traditional office layout.
[ ] I want a less traditional office.
[ ] I want to work with the latest technologies.
[ ] I need to feel connected to my coworkers.
[ ] I need to feel connected to my bosses.
[ ] Internal communication is important to me.
[ ] I need for people to listen to my ideas.
[ ] I want to feel company spirit.
[ ] I want to have friends at work.

## Leadership and Working Styles

[ ] I want a laid-back boss.
[ ] I want a coach.
[ ] I want a mentor.
[ ] I want a taskmaster.
[ ] I need to be pushed to get all my work done.
[ ] I want to be left to complete projects in my own ways.
[ ] I want to like my boss.
[ ] I want to respect my boss.
[ ] I want for my boss to respect my opinion.
[ ] I want a much less formal relationship with the people above me.
[ ] I prefer traditional leader/employee relationships.
[ ] I want to feel like my coworkers are happy in their jobs.
[ ] I want my boss to be highly accessible.
[ ] I want to feel like I can ask my leaders anything.
[ ] I want to feel like I can always talk to my boss.
[ ] I want to be able to voice concerns easily and safely.
[ ] I want to be able to offer suggestions about how to do things better.
[ ] I want a lot of responsibility in my next job.
[ ] I don't want a lot of responsibility.
[ ] I want successes to be my responsibility and failures to be my fault.
[ ] I want the company to be open to change.
[ ] Open working environments suit me best.
[ ] I want a more traditional office/cubicle working area.
[ ] I want opportunities for promotion.
[ ] I want opportunities for transfer.
[ ] I need to feel like the company wants me.
[ ] I want the company to have minimal office politics.

## Environment

[ ] Location is important to me.
[ ] I want to work downtown.
[ ] I want to work uptown.

# SCORESHEETS 171

[ ] I want to work in a rural area.
[ ] I want to work in the suburbs.
[ ] I want to work in _____.
[ ] I need to be out of the office on a regular basis.
[ ] I want to travel.
[ ] I need the workplace to be close to the interstate.
[ ] I need access to public transportation.
[ ] I want to be close to home.
[ ] I want to be able to walk to work.
[ ] I want to be able to bike to work.
[ ] I want employee carpools.
[ ] I would be willing to move or transfer to another office.
[ ] I would be willing to move or relocate to another city or state.
[ ] I need a 9 to 5 schedule.
[ ] I want to work the _____ to _____ shift.
[ ] I want to work _____ hours per week.
[ ] I need/want to work from home some of the time.
[ ] I need/want to work from home all of the time.
[ ] I need/want to telecommute.
[ ] I want a better quality of work life.
[ ] I want to spend no more than _____ hours per week at work.
[ ] I want to spend no fewer than _____ hours per week at home.
[ ] I want to work in an office.
[ ] I can work in cubicles.
[ ] I refuse to work in cubicles.
[ ] I like traditional office layouts.
[ ] I would be interested in an open office.
[ ] I need to be able to personalize my workspace.
[ ] I want to work in teams.
[ ] I want to work alone.
[ ] I want to work directly for someone else.
[ ] I need to be able to get away from the office for breaks.
[ ] I need on-site break areas.
[ ] I need on-site or close-by eating opportunities.

[ ] I want modern facilities and the latest equipment and technology.
[ ] I want to work at a desk.
[ ] I want to work where I'll be around people.
[ ] I want to work on the sales floor.
[ ] I want to work in assembly.
[ ] I want a window.
[ ] I want to work outside.
[ ] I want to work inside.
[ ] I want my job to be different every day.
[ ] I would be willing to wear a uniform.
[ ] I would be willing to wear a suit every day.
[ ] I need a "blue jeans" environment.

## Benefits

[ ] I need basic health insurance.
[ ] I need expanded health insurance.

I want/need the following coverage:

[ ] Dental
[ ] Vision
[ ] Maternal/paternal
[ ] Mental health
[ ] I want/need special insurance options.
[ ] I want creative insurance options, such as pet insurance.
[ ] I want group auto insurance.
[ ] I want group homeowners/renters insurance.
[ ] I need benefits extended to domestic partners.
[ ] I want maternal/paternal leave.
[ ] I want to be able to work part-time or contractually and still have benefits options.
[ ] I want health benefits beyond insurance.
[ ] I need wellness programs.
[ ] I need health club membership options.
[ ] I want retirement programs.
[ ] I want savings programs.

# SCORESHEETS

[ ] I want investment programs.
[ ] I want _____ weeks of vacation.
[ ] I must have the ability to take _____ holidays.
[ ] I want my vacation and sick days to carry over.
[ ] I'm looking for _____ sick days.
[ ] I want the opportunity to take sabbaticals.
[ ] I need on-site childcare.
[ ] I need some sort of subsidized childcare.
[ ] I need emergency childcare for snow days and the like.
[ ] I need elder care and/or dependent care options.
[ ] I want creative benefits choices, like the chance to bring my pet to work, or _____.
[ ] I want side benefits like perks, discounts, tickets, reward programs, or _____.
[ ] I want my employer to pay for all or part of my education.
[ ] I want the chance to earn _____ degree while I'm working.
[ ] I need or want the following benefit: _____.

## Compensation

[ ] I must make $_____ per week/month/year.
[ ] I would like to make $_____ per week/month/year.
[ ] I think a realistic goal for compensation is $_____, and I won't take less money than that.
[ ] I want to receive a raise in _____ months.
[ ] The pay of jobs above me is important to me.
[ ] I want to be promoted in _____ months.
[ ] I want pay to increase as my responsibility does.
[ ] I want the financial package to be competitive with industry norms.
[ ] I would be willing to consider items other than money as part of the overall compensation package.
[ ] Overtime payment is important to me.
[ ] Bonus structures are important to me.
[ ] I want a year-end bonus.

[ ] I want a signing bonus.
[ ] I want performance-based bonuses.
[ ] I want to have a regular salary.
[ ] I prefer to work on commission or a pay-for-performance basis.
[ ] I want to be able to receive equity in the company.
[ ] I want profit-sharing options.
[ ] I want stock options.
[ ] I want savings and retirement funds.
[ ] I want to feel like the pay is worth the job. That number is: _____ .

## Intangibles

[ ] I want my work to be meaningful.
[ ] I want to find a deeper purpose in my work.
[ ] I want to make a positive difference in the world.
[ ] I want to make a positive difference in my community.
[ ] I want to be able to see the results of my work.
[ ] I want to be doing what *I* want to do.
[ ] I want to pursue my dream job.
[ ] I want to get paid for doing what I love.
[ ] I've always wanted to _____.
[ ] I want to be doing _____ in six months, in a year, in five years, in ten years.
[ ] I want challenging work.
[ ] I want difficult work.
[ ] I want to have to find new solutions every day.
[ ] My work must be rewarding.
[ ] I need to have a clear idea of what would be required in the job I'm considering.
[ ] I want the work I do to be mine.
[ ] I want credit for my work.
[ ] I want recognition for a job well done.
[ ] I want to feel appreciated in my next job.
[ ] I want a company concerned with giving back to the community.

# SCORESHEETS

[ ] I want opportunities to enhance civic life in my next job.
[ ] I want to work for a responsible corporate citizen.
[ ] I want to work for a socially conscious company.
[ ] I want to work for a company that espouses these social and political views: _____.
[ ] I want volunteer opportunities in my next job.
[ ] I want my job to make my life more meaningful.
[ ] I want a better work/life balance.
[ ] I want to love my job.
[ ] I want to have fun.

## WORKSHEET ONE

List all of the items that you scored a +5. These are the things you really need to focus on in your job search. *Once you have listed these items, work to weave them into a paragraph or two about what you need out of your next job.* In that way, you'll have a more concise idea of what you are looking for. When the time comes to articulate those wants/needs to a potential employer, you'll already have them written down once—so you won't be saying it for the first time. You will also want to list all of your -5 items—those things you really want to avoid in your next job.

**List +5 Items Here**

_____
_____
_____
_____
_____
_____
_____
_____
_____
_____
_____
_____
_____

# WORKSHEETS

**List -5 Items Here**

APPENDIX A

**Use this page to write out the description of your ideal job in words:**

## WORKSHEET TWO

List all of your +4 and +3 items, and do the same with your -3 and -4 scores. These items will still be important in your job search. Writing them down again will help you keep them fresh in your mind as you begin your search. Items that you have scored between -2 and +2 may still be important, but they will not necessarily be deciding factors in the process.

## WORKSHEET THREE

We've provided several worksheets for you to fill out about your previous jobs to help you evaluate what you liked and disliked about those positions. After all, you are the expert on what works and doesn't work *for you*. If you need more sheets than those that we've provided here, simply make copies as necessary.

Job: _____

My title: _____

My job responsibilities included:
_____
_____
_____
_____

My wages/salary: $ _____ / month / year

The compensation was fair/not fair because:
_____
_____

Things I really liked about the job:
_____
_____

Things I did not like about the job:
_____
_____
_____

# WORKSHEETS

I wish I'd had the chance to:
_____
_____

The people I worked with were:
_____
_____

I would/would not like to find people like that again.

I liked the way(s) my boss . . .
_____
_____
_____

I really did not like the way my boss . . .
_____
_____
_____

Things I want to do in my next job that I did in this job:
_____
_____
_____

Things I'll never do again:
_____
_____
_____
_____

Use your answers here in conjunction with your answers from the scoresheets to help you continue to hone in on exactly what you're looking for.

# Appendix B

## Sabbaticals

Almost everyone is familiar with the notion of sabbaticals. For years instructors and professors in academia have been rewarded for time spent teaching in colleges and universities with several weeks, months, or even a full year of time away from their jobs. In today's increasingly fast-paced and, of course, ever more stressful marketplace, the popularity of sabbaticals is spreading from the academic world to the business world.

While in the past few years and even decades some forward-looking companies have provided sabbaticals or mini-sabbaticals—which we'll address in a moment—for their upper-level management, this trend is being pushed down the corporate ladder. Sabbaticals are becoming more and more available—not just for elite employees, but for workers at every level.

### First Things First

*Just what is a sabbatical, and how does the concept translate to the business world?* A sabbatical, simply put, is an extended time away from your job—without risk of losing that job. Depending on the situation, your salary may continue or may be suspended, benefits may or may not continue, but your job security certainly continues. Essentially, you get to take a break from your job, from your work, and then come back to your job refreshed, recharged, and reenergized.

Academics have long taken semesters or years off in order to pursue their own work, or simply to take time away from the classroom. This way, when they return, they will once again have the spark needed to perform to the highest level possible. The same concept translates to the business arena. After a while, even in the best jobs, the work and stress can pile up to the point where some of the fun might be missing, where the rewards don't seem to quite match up to the effort required. This, after all, is why we take vacations—in fact, it's why we have weekends! No one can work *all the time*. We need time away.

A sabbatical of weeks, months, or, at the longest, a year (we don't recommend pursuing a sabbatical of a longer period of time; you'll lose your edge) can give you what vacations can't: A period of time away from your job, away from your desk, of a length sufficient for you to refocus on your job, your career, your goals, and your life.

We forecast that the sabbatical will become as common and widespread in coming years as health insurance is now. Whether between jobs or simply taking a break from a current job, we anticipate that employees will take significant amounts of time to refocus—every eight to ten years. The sabbatical is the wave of the future, whether self- or employer-funded.

## Planning Your Leave

*How can I plan for my own sabbatical?* Planning, in fact, is the key component to opening the doors to sabbatical opportunities. Many companies may allow for sabbaticals, but may not fund them. If you work for such a company, you should begin saving for such an event years before you actually plan to take the time off. If, for instance, you want to take a year-long sabbatical, you should save 10 percent of your income for ten years in order to maintain your current standard of living. It's important that you can afford to maintain your desired living standard; if you must concentrate too heavily on whether you'll be able to pay your bills, you will be defeating the purpose of the sabbatical in the first place—relaxing.

The bottom line: Make sure that you can *afford* to take the time off when the time comes.

## The ABCs of AARP

*What about retirement?* There is another aspect to the concept of sabbaticals that we haven't yet mentioned. We expect retirement, as we now know it, to disappear altogether within about 20 years. People will simply choose not to retire at all, or at least not completely.

If you believe that you are unlikely ever to want to retire, you may choose not to set aside so large a nest egg. But be careful. You'll still need some money, some savings, in case you choose to cut back to part-time employment in your senior years.

## Making Sense of Sabbaticals

*How does this translate to my job search?* If you are looking to make a long-term commitment to a company, you may well want to include the possibility of a sabbatical as one of your selection criteria. Do not be reluctant to discuss these sorts of benefits in interview situations. It is likely, in fact, that discussing the possibility of staying with an employer for eight to ten years may be to your benefit in the interview process. You'll appear to be well-informed and clearly focused.

Remember, just like all the other criteria discussed in this book, *you* are in charge of your own future. If you are intrigued by and interested in the possibility of taking a sabbatical, do your homework *before* you begin speaking to different employers. The possibilities are out there for you—you just have to seek them out.

# Appendix C

## Self-Employment

Are you one of those many people who has dreams of being his or her own boss? Imagine what it might be like: You set your schedule; you decide about vacations, benefits, salary; you have direct control and responsibility for successes and failures... the business would be *yours*. This dream may not be as far away as you might think.

As the workforce becomes more and more fragmented and skills become more and more specialized, working for yourself is becoming not only a more attractive option, but a more viable one as well.

Companies are often looking for solutions to short-term needs, services that they would rather pay for on an as-needed basis rather than through salary, or simply outside contractors. Think for a moment about the skills and abilities you possess. Would you better serve yourself by striking out on your own?

### Making You Work for You

*How can you find a way to be self-employed?* There seem to be as many options for self-employment as there are services to be offered. We'll cover a few of them here:

- **Contracting:** This option is as straightforward as it sounds. You simply agree to contract your services to a firm for a set rate. From high-level stock market forecasting to dry-wall installation, almost anyone can become a contractor.

In fact, as we continue here, much of what we'll discuss will involve some form of contracting. Whether you choose to be paid hourly or by the job is up to you, but treat the transaction as you would any other sale in any other arena. You're selling your services to them. Make sure the agreement is beneficial to both parties. As a contractor, you will operate as an independent business, with responsibility for paying taxes and other legal obligations.

- **Consulting:** Consulting is essentially a form of contracting for knowledge-based skills. You are selling your expertise to a company that needs your advice. Remember that even though you are being brought in as a "guru" of sorts, you don't want to present yourself as being too cocky. Be reasonable and respectful at all times, and remember that you have sold your services and your knowledge to the client—and that "customer service" can be a big part of both a successful sale and repeat business. Be sure you find a common ground where you can be happy in your work and the company will be happy with your results.

- **Freelancing:** Again, freelance work is a form of contracting, though freelance workers most often work for more than one company at a time on smaller projects. Though the term seems to be most often applied to writers who have multiple irons in multiple fires, you can freelance virtually any skill. It's simply a matter of marketing yourself and your abilities in the right way.

- **Short-term or project work:** An option that is gaining popularity in the workplace is that of signing on with an organization for a set (short) period of time. You contract for a month, or two, or six, or even for a year or more, for a specific task. You are engaged to complete a job. Once it's completed, you move on to the next assignment, perhaps at a different company altogether. This option can be very attractive for someone who does not want to be tied down

# SELF-EMPLOYMENT

to a specific job or company indefinitely, or for someone who is unsure about what he or she wants to be doing.

## But Watch Out. . .

There are a few things to be aware of when striking out on your own. We don't mean to suggest that we've covered it all here, either—whole books and series of books have been written on this subject, and if you're interested in being self-employed you should spend a bit of time in your local bookstore or library to see what's out there. Just a few words of caution, though, on being your own boss:

1. Make sure you have enough of a monetary cushion to last you through the tough times, should you hit a stretch where there isn't any business for a while. Advance planning is key.
2. Have a complete business plan. Make sure that you know how to handle both a lack of business and an explosion of business (the latter is often overlooked).
3. Make sure you keep taxes in mind. Don't get caught in April with a huge tax bill.

Being your own boss can be one of the most rewarding things you can do for yourself. If you've got the skills and the courage, go for it!

# Appendix D

## *Temporary Work and Temp-to-Hire*

Everything in our culture these days is instant—instant coffee, instant cereal, and instant rice. Employers want their world to be instant as well—instant profits, instant turnaround, and, for the past few decades, instant workers. The staffing industry grew out of these desires. Employers have a need that they want filled immediately, and staffing services can provide the people to fill that need.

But the benefit does not rest solely with the employers. Staffing services are on the rise in today's society, and not just because employers have more needs. Some employees find these temporary staffing firms valuable resources both in their careers and in their job searches.

Though "temp" work has traditionally focused on clerical and light industrial tasks, as the needs of the marketplace change, the staffing industry is becoming much more diverse. Modern staffing firms still offer light industrial and secretarial workers, but they now offer professional and technical workers to employers as well. In addition, some staffing firms seek out and place workers in such diverse fields as law, accounting, programming, systems analysis, executive positions, and technical troubleshooting. Today's staffing firms are nothing like the old "Kelly Girls" image of the middle of the century.

## Considering Staffing Firms

*Why You Should Consider a Staffing Firm in Your Job Search:* Many people shy away from staffing firms as they begin their job searches, but you should look carefully at the advantages temporary work may hold for you. We'll discuss several of them here.

- **Temporary work:** While it may seem obvious, one of the biggest advantages of temporary work is just that: It is temporary. You're not tied down to any one job for a great length of time. The flexibility of temp jobs is among their most alluring qualities. Most temporary positions range from a few days all the way up to eight weeks, with the majority of placements falling in the three to five week range. Essentially, if you want to, need to, or can afford to, you can work a month, then take a week off between each job. The reasons behind this design range from a simple desire for flexibility to family obligations, but having the option not to work for any given length of time is certainly a bonus.

- **Ease in finding a job:** In essence, the staffing firm will handle your job search for you. It's *their* job. You simply provide them with your resume and applicable skills, perhaps take a few proficiency tests, and they place you where they believe you'll best fit. You can walk in the door of a staffing firm on a Monday and go to work on Tuesday.

- **Opportunity to try different jobs:** Since most appointments range from a week to a month, you'll have the opportunity to work in many different work environments. At the very least, you'll learn where you work the best and where you'd rather not work. This kind of multiple assignment experience may be a good way for you to learn what kind of working environment you prefer.

- **Temp-to-hire:** Temp agencies have one of the highest rates of employee turnover in the business—a statistic that might seem like a drawback until you look closer. In some firms,

# TEMPORARY WORK AND TEMP-TO-HIRE

the rate of temp workers being hired on a permanent basis by the companies they have been placed with is as high as 70 percent. All the benefits available to you, in terms of finding work easily, grow exponentially when you consider that the staffing firm may not only find you a job, but, in fact, a *permanent* job. Temp agencies can actually handle your job search for you . . . and you'll even get to audition the company, the job responsibilities, your coworkers, and the culture *before* you commit to permanent assignment.

## A Few Things to Know

Most temporary staffing firms pay hourly fees, and the pay, of course, depends largely on your ability and the level of work you are performing. Usually the pay is quite competitive with industry standards. While job security and benefits may not be high, some temp firms offer vacation, retirement, and a few even offer some form of health insurance. These types of benefits change from firm to firm, so be sure that (as we've said everywhere else in this book) you do your homework. The more you know about any situation—temp work or otherwise—the more likely you are to find happiness in your next job.

As in any situation, there are benefits as well as drawbacks to temporary work. You may trade salaried pay for flexibility. You may trade security for variety. However, if you're not sure what to do next, or if you're not sure how long you want to work next week (or even if you want to work next week!), or even if you just feel the job search to be a bit overwhelming, temporary work may be for you.

> *Information for this appendix came in part from an interview with Don Stallard, CEO of The Reserves Network, a temporary staffing firm with offices in Ohio, North Carolina, South Carolina, Kentucky, and Florida. The Reserves Network employed, at one time or another last year, over 15,000 people, and has more than 4,000 people employed at any given time. For more information, go to www.reservesnet.com.*

# Appendix E

## On-Line Job Hunting

As the Internet becomes a tool of the masses, not of just academics and technology experts, more and more business is actually being done on-line. Naturally, a greater number of employment want ads are appearing there as well. Don't limit your search for your next job to just newspaper classified ads. Look on the various job boards that the Internet has to offer. You'll get the chance to tailor your search to your needs, and, perhaps most importantly, you'll send a message to any employers you contact that *you're web literate*. Responding electronically can be one of the most important first impressions you can make.

We've listed a few of the biggest Internet job sites here, and, when possible, provided a brief summary of what's available on each site. We recommend that you go to several and then choose one or two or three that will be of most use to you.

## America's Job Bank (*www.jobsearch.com*)

This site is free to employers and is a partnership between the U.S. Department of Labor and various state employment agencies. It has been vastly improved since coming on-line some years ago, and is now well-built and easily understood. It links to a variety of other job search and job assistance Websites, and offers categorized linking options to users.

## Career Builder Network (www.careerbuilder.com)

While there is no means for posting resumes, this site features companies regularly and has other interesting links such as job-hunting tips and various job search articles and information. The site will e-mail you when jobs you have specified are posted.

## CareerPath (careerpath.com)

This Website combines listings from various employers' Websites as well as help wanted listings from newspapers across the country. No one job listing stays on the site for more than two weeks, which serves to alleviate the traditional pitfalls of applying for a job that has already been filled. You can search by salary level along with the traditional sorting devices. CareerPath also offers regular prize giveaways.

## HeadHunter.net (www.headhunter.net)

Linked, among other sites, to jobsearch.com, HeadHunter.net is becoming quite popular among employers on a budget due to its $20 job-posting fee. What this means to you is that there are a lot of jobs here to look at; 185,000 jobs were listed in January 2000 and the site had 3.3 million hits. This site is a bit more focused toward employers, but it's worth a few minutes of your time.

## HotJobs.com (www.hotjobs.com)

This site has a "no headhunters" policy, which, along with souped-up graphics and a hot national image and reputation, serves to make it among the Web's most popular sites for job seekers. Search options include keyword, job, location, and company entries. This site is interesting because, among other job categorizations, it includes "entry-level" and "start-

# ON-LINE JOB HUNTING

up" search options. The board also features sweepstakes and giveaways.

### Jobs Online (www.getajob.com)

Upbeat graphics and text make this site user friendly. It features a Job Aptitude Test that can help those seeking to switch career paths or simply enhance current ones.

### JobOptions (www.joboptions.com)

An employment Website for all fields and categories, the prime attraction of JobOptions may be the ease of submitting resumés. It also features a personalized e-mail Job Alert option in which the site will e-mail you each time a job fitting your specifications is posted. Resumé builder programs and links on the site are a nice bonus.

### Jobs.com (www.jobs.com)

This fast and user-friendly site focuses each job searcher to major cities and geographical areas across the U.S. It offers searches by job categories, and the opportunity to search employer lists. The site holds on-line career fairs and lists career fairs in your area. Jobs.com also has special links for students and first-time job seekers.

### Jobtrak.com (www.jobtrak.com)

Jobtrak is the largest job listing/resume posting service targeted specifically to college students and recent graduates. The site and database are password-protected and can only be accessed by the students and alumni of partnered institutions. It offers job listings as well as scholarship searches. The site provides links to companies as well as links to savings opportunities outside of your job search—which can be valuable if you're on a budget!

## Monster.com (www.monster.com)

Monster is easily one of the biggest (if not *the* biggest) job board on the Web. It's also one of the hippest. Flashy graphics and quick linking times make this site particularly appealing. While the focus is primarily on tech jobs, a variety of jobs are listed and updated frequently. You can sign up for a free e-mail newsletter about job hunting, and you can register on the site, so that each time you visit your search is personalized. There are more than 315,000 jobs listed, and there is an opportunity to post your resume to headhunters as well. One of the most interesting site features is a virtual career fair boasting more than 1500 pages of career advice.

## N2Hiring (www.n2hiring.com)

Afraid your current employer may discover that you're on the market? Be sure to check out N2Hiring. Though as we go to press the site is in its infancy, we believe that it will be a primo spot to begin your IT job search. Developed by folks who really understand your concerns, N2Hiring does not require you to give your real name *until you want to actually apply for a job*. They even facilitate your getting an anonymous e-mail address on Yahoo, Excite!, or Hotmail. You plug in that address and your qualifications; they do the rest. Whenever an opening for which you qualify is posted to their site, they'll e-mail you at your anonymous address and invite you to apply for the job. So, your confidentiality is maintained until *you're* ready to get serious.

## And Remember . . . (www.yourhometown, search engines, etc.)

Look to the on-line arms of local and regional newspapers and magazines where you live. They may have links to local and national job boards, and employers may advertise there before anywhere else. Other good places to consider include

# ON-LINE JOB HUNTING 199

major search engines like Lycos, Yahoo, and HotBot, which may have their own employment listings or at least links to job boards. Keep in mind that a job board is only as good as the people and organizations using it, and each is focused slightly differently. Spend a few minutes looking at a few of the above that seem to suit you—and then begin your on-line search. Good luck and happy surfing!

# Index

## A

abilities, leadership, 36
accessibility, 62
Adopt-a-Highway, 134
adoption, 93
Allied Signal, 63
America's Job Bank, 195
American Express, 97, 99
American Red Cross, 131
Ames Rubber, 104
appreciation, 128–129
Arco, 99
Arizona Mail Order, 131
Ash, Mary Kay, 64
Ask Yourself, 4, 16, 17, 19–23, 37, 54, 68, 72, 86, 106, 119, 137
Avon Products, 99

## B

background,
 educational, 5
 personal, 5
Bakken, Earl, 130
Bank of America, 36
BankBoston, 98
bean stock, 118

Ben & Jerry's, 101
benefits, 21, 89–108
   family friendly, 82
   financial, 96
   health, 94
   maternal/paternal, 93
   nonpay-related, 114
   options, 21
Boddie-Noell, 136
bonus(es), 23, 74, 89, 96, 102, 115, 117, 120, 144, 157, 158, 173, 174, 192, 197
   company-based, 115
   contractor, 116
   employee-based performance, 116
   signing, 116
   tenure-based, 116
   year-end, 115
boss(es), 18, 19, 47, 49, 51, 54, 57–58, 60–62, 64, 67–68, 96, 145, 153, 163–165, 169–170, 181, 187, 189
   making friends with
   types of
      coach, the, 59
      friend, the, 58
      mentor, the, 59
      taskmaster, the, 59
      traditional, the, 59
Bossidy, Larry, 63
Boy/Girl Scouts of America, vi, 131
break areas, 20, 81, 86, 155, 171
Bright Horizons Family Solutions, 84, 99
Brink's Home Security, 133
budget worksheet, 112
Burrell Cancer Institute, 132
Burrell Professional labs, 132
business plan, 189

# INDEX

## C

Career Builder Network, 196
career, 3
  destiny, 147
  fairs, on-line, 197, 198
  path, 148, 197
CareerPath, 196
CDW, 66
challenged, being, 126, 137
challenging work, 158, 174
chambers of commerce, 114, 131
Chevron, 99
Child Development Center, 98
childcare, 84, 93, 97, 106, 112
  backup, 98
    Bank Boston Snowy Day Program, 98–99
    ChildrenFirst, 99
  emergency, 157, 173
  on-site, 22, 98, 157, 173
  subsidized, 157, 173
children, 84, 98–99, 132
  adoption of, 93
  exploitation of, 132
  making their wishes come true, 135
  summer camp for, 84
  underprivileged, 133, 136
ChildrenFirst, 99
choices, ix, xi–xii, 22, 24, 29, 31–32, 71–72, 90, 97, 101, 116, 144, 157, 173
choosing an industry, 29
CIGNA, 105
  CIGNA-Penn program, 105
  Group Insurance, 105
coach, 19, 58, 59
coaching, 5, 131
Coach University, v

Colgate-Palmolive, 99
Comet Pay, 80
commissions, 117
communications, internal, 18, 50, 54, 62, 153, 169
community, 35, 72, 114, 125, 129, 138
   assistance, 134
   business, 33, 43
   cleanups, 134
   college, 104
   concern about, 138
   corporate, 34
   giving back to the, 159, 174
   leader, 38
   local, 23, 131
   newspapers, 72
   making a difference for the, 125, 137, 158, 174
   outreach, 24
   participation, 35
   reputation, 34
   service, 5, 22, 97, 133, 135–136
   service day, 135
   theatre, 102
commuting, 20, 73, 111
   dilemmas, 74
   options benefits, 22
   tele-, 20, 72–73, 75–76
company, the
   culture, 17
   type of, 15
company-based performance, 115
compensation, 6, 89, 109–122, 157–158, 164, 173–174, 180
   bonuses, 115–116
   choices, 22
   commissions, 117
   equity, 117
   options, 23
   other payment choices, 116–117

# INDEX

    package(s), 21, 74, 77, 94, 97, 116, 118–119
    profit-related pay, 117
    profit sharing, 117
    stock options, 117
competitive pay, 113
Conde Nast, 99
consulting, 188, 204
contracting, 187–188
contractor, 23, 116, 188
copay, 90, 91, 95
corporate,
  recess, 82
  spirit, 51
  stability, 31
criteria for selection, 7, 15–25
cubicle(s), 12, 78, 86, 154, 155, 171
    creature, 20, 78
    forest, 18
    partitions, 49
    working area, 170
daddies, 93
Datatel, Inc., 102–103, 135
    Scholars Foundation, 135
Deloitte & Touche, 99
dependent care, 98, 106, 157, 173
    childcare, 22, 93, 97–99, 106, 112, 157, 173
    elder care, 22, 106, 157, 173
    pet care, 22, 91–92
discounts, 52, 74, 101, 157, 173
    pet care, 92
doggie day care, 100
    Justice Telecom, 100
domestic partner, 92, 106, 156
    benefits, 92, 156
dress code, 54
Duck Challenge Day, 53
Dupont, 97

## E

Edelman Group, The, 118
Edelman, Terri, 118
education, 106
   continuing, 103–105
   field-related, 22
education reimbursement program, 105
educational,
   background, 5
   benefit programs, 105
   costs, 104
   opportunities, 103
   skills, 5
Elizabeth Glaser Pediatric AIDS Foundation, 132
emergency,
   childcare, 98, 106, 157, 173
   closing at the childcare center, 99
   in case of, 111
   response, 135
   veterinary care, 92
Emerson Electric, 84
employee-centered, work environments, 129
Employer of Choice$^{SM}$, 110
English as a Second Language (ESL), 104
environment(s), 6, 10, 36, 42, 46, 49, 63, 65, 96, 100, 124, 138, 150, 154–155, 170–171
   alternative, 83
   "blue jeans", 156, 172
   cleaning up the, 134
   collaborative team, 19
   employee-centered, 129
   home-like, 78
   open office, 18, 164, 170
   physical, 77–78
   relaxed, 61
   social, 20, 83

# INDEX

unsafe, 83
work(ing), 12, 19–20, 47, 68, 71–88, 147, 192
environmentally friendly, 134
equality, 43, 54, 153, 169
  age-based, 54, 153, 169
  based on sexual orientation, 54, 153, 169
  gender-based, 54, 153, 169
  racial, 54, 153, 169
equity, 117, 120, 158, 174
  in work/life balance, 77
  options, 23
ethics and honesty, 17, 43, 54, 153, 169
expectations, 127–128, 137
  payment for exceeding, 115–116
  job, 5–6
experience,
  career-specific, 5
  leadership, 5
  management, 5
  people-specific, 5
  valuing, 44

## F

family friendly,
  benefits, 82
  events, 83
  policies, 83
flexible office layout, 80
flextime, 6, 20, 22, 74–75
  home/office, 75
  traditional, 75
  virtual office, the, 75
flexibility, 19, 74, 77, 83, 192
  temp jobs, of, 192
  trade salaried pay for, 193
  working hours, in, 133

formality, 60–61
   workplace, 47, 81, 85
Founder's Day, 135
free ticket program, 102
freelancing, 188
friend(s), 53, 55, 58, 68, 83, 130, 135, 145, 148, 153, 169
   making, 63–64
   recruit(ing), 45, 144
   the, type of boss, 19, 58, 60
friendship(s), 20, 46, 68
Fuerstein, Aaron, 129
fundraising, 134, 136

## G

Gallup, Patricia, 63, 93–94
George, Bill, 130
Gillette, 99
Glickman, David, 100
greenspace, 134
Gymboree, 82

## H

Hallmark, 97
Hardee's Restaurants, 136
having fun, 45, 145–146, 149–150
HeadHunter.net, 196
health club memberships, 95, 156, 172
kids, helping, 84, 98, 134
   program(s), 84, 131, 133
      HA-LO Kids Heaven, 133
      Kids-at-Work days, 134
      Summer Time Kids Camp, 84
Herman Group, The, 103
hideouts, 81

# INDEX

highway cleanups, 134
*Hot Tips*, 12, 30, 32, 37, 42, 45, 47, 50, 60, 65, 67, 73, 74, 77, 78, 83, 85, 95, 103, 114, 125–126, 127, 136
HotJobs.com, 196
Hudson Institute, The, 43

## I

income,
  desired, 111
  future, 113
  levels in the community, 114
  net, 112
  present, 113
  saving a percentage of, 111, 184
insurance, 89, 114
  adoptive parents, for, 93
  auto, 106, 112, 156, 172
  choices, 90–92
  CIGNA Group, 105
  dental, 91, 156, 172
  health, 21, 93, 95, 156, 172, 184, 193
  homeowners/renters, 156, 172
  hospitalization, 90
  legal, 106
  life, 91
  major medical, 90
  mental health, 156, 172
  other, 91
  pet, 11, 12, 92, 106, 156, 172
  routine health, 90
  special options, 156, 172
  vision, 91, 156, 172
intangibles, 10, 23, 24, 123–139, 146, 158–159, 174–175
Intel, 97
InTouch, 55

## J

job expectations, 5
JobOptions, 197
Jobs Online, 197
Jobs.com, 197
Jobtrak.com, 197
Jordana, Rosemary, 99
Justice Telecom, 100

## K

Kahl, Jack, 53
KinderCare, 97
Kiwanis, 131
Krasny, Michael, 66
Kroger, 35

## L

La Petite, 97
leadership, vi, 5, 9, 18–19, 57–69, 71, 89, 127, 154, 157, 170
   abilities, 36
   open style, 93
   styles, 58–60
length of stay, 6–7
Leonard, Thomas, v
life balance, vi, 19, 76, 103, 148, 159, 175
location(s), 20, 71–72, 73, 86, 154, 170, 196
   remote, 48
logo apparel, 101
lottery tickets, 52

## M

making a difference, 124–125, 129
making the choice, 7, 29–141

# INDEX

Malden Mills Industries, 129
Management Communications Systems, Inc., 55
Manco, Inc., 53
market(s),
  changing, xi, 144
  job, 57
  leader, 16, 33, 141, 167
  labor, 90
  position, 16, 33–34, 152, 168
  share, 16, 33, 141, 167
  talent-short, 31
  today's, 145, 146
  value, your, 113
marketable skills, 4–5, 149
marketing,
  department, 63
  internal, 50
  yourself, 4–5, 188
marketplace, 103
  conditions, 65
  current, 147
  ever-changing, 6, 21, 79
  needs of changing, 191
  stressful, 183
  today's, 74, 92
Mary Kay Cosmetics, 64
Mastery Works, Inc., 62
Mayes, William P. "Phil", 126
Medtronic, 130
membership, gym or health club, 95, 106, 156, 172
mentor(s), v, xiii, 54, 59, 68, 135, 154, 170
mentoring, 134, 153, 169
MGM Transport Corporation, 48
Microsoft, 97
Modern International Graphics, 52
mommies, 93

monetary cushion, 189
money, 22, 23, 52, 79, 89, 105, 109–120, 157–158, 173–174, 185
  raising, 134
Monster.com, 198
Motek, 75

## N

N2Hiring, 198
Netscape, 100
Noble & Associates, 79–80
Noble, Bob, 79
nutrition programs, 95
nutritional guidance, 106

## O

on-line job hunting, 195–199
on-site,
  break areas, 155, 171
  cafeteria, 95
  childcare, 22, 98, 157, 173
  cost manager, 83
  gyms, 95
  learning opportunities, 22
  pet care, 21, 22, 100
  services, 22, 102, 106
openness to change, 65
opportunities, ix, 17, 22, 24, 30, 35, 66, 105, 125, 131, 132, 134, 159
  career, 6, 62
  compensation, 119
  eating, 20, 81, 155, 171
  educational, 103
  employment, 61
  for advancement, 113

# INDEX

    for promotion, 154, 170
    for transfer, 154, 170
    future, 19
    growth, 6
    learning, 22
    profit sharing, 23
    rewarding, 133
    savings, 197
    to make a difference, 124, 131–137
    volunteer, 35, 36, 133–137, 159, 175
Opryland Hotel, 98
overtime, 23, 115, 120, 157, 173
ownership, 24, 128

## P

part-time(rs), 93, 94, 106, 156, 172
    workers, 21
Patrice Tanaka & Company, Inc., 135
pay, 109–120, 157–158, 173–174
    Comet Pay, 80
    competitive, 113–114
    for parking, 73
    for performance, 23, 102, 116, 118, 158, 174
    profit-related, 117
    salary vs. hourly, 23
    scales, 114, 115, 119
    to increase as responsibility does, 157, 173
payment
    car, 112
    choices, other, 116
    options, 116, 120
PC Connection, 63, 93
penny-pinching, 110
performance,
    employee-based, 116
    pay for, 23, 102, 116, 118, 158, 174

perks, 52, 89, 105, 106, 157, 173
  local 102
Pet Assure, 92
  pet care, on-site, 21, 22, 100
pet-friendly workplaces, 22
pet(s), 21, 22, 91, 92, 100
"piggyback" plan, 90
planning,
  for your future, 6
  your leave, 184–185
  to start or increase your family, 93
  to stay, 6, 149
policies, 18, 21, 43, 91, 100
  domestic partner, 106
  employee-oriented, 66
  family friendly, 83
  pet-friendly, 101
Professional Photographers Association Charities, 132
profit sharing, 23, 117, 118, 158, 174
profit-related pay, 117
project work, 188–189
promotions, 23, 50, 66–67, 115, 119
quality, 5, 16, 36, 42–43, 58, 76, 130, 152, 153, 168, 169
  employers, 83
  importance of, 36, 38, 54, 152, 168, 169
  leadership, 89
  of people, 45
  of service, 54

## R

raise(s), 22, 113, 119, 157, 173
  getting a, 113
Real-World Practices, 11, 34, 35, 36, 43, 44, 46, 48, 51, 52, 53, 62, 63, 64, 66, 76, 79, 82, 84, 92, 93, 86, 97, 98, 99, 100–101, 102, 103, 104, 105, 114, 118, 126, 129, 130, 131, 132, 135, 136

# INDEX

relationship(s), 19, 58–64, 68, 109, 145, 153, 154, 169, 170
researching the company, 32
Reserves Network, The, 193
results, 23, 43, 44, 51, 92, 125, 128, 137, 158, 188
retirement, 21, 44, 89, 96, 106, 117, 120, 156, 158, 172, 174, 185, 193
reward(s), 32, 97, 115, 117, 126,
   bonuses, 115–116
   for innovation, 18, 48–49
   long-term, 118
   profit sharing, 117
   programs, 52, 54, 102, 106, 115
rewarding, 135
   genius, 48–49, 54
   ingenuity and new ideas, 127
   jobs, 127, 137, 145, 146
   work, 158, 174
Richter, Leon, 100
right job, finding the, 127
Rotary Clubs, 131

## S

sabbaticals, 97, 106, 157, 173, 183–185
safety record, 20, 71, 83
Sara Lee, 99
Save the Children, 131
savings, 21, 106, 111, 112, 119, 120, 156, 158, 172, 174, 185
   pet-care program, 92
   plans, 96
Schwartz, Carol, 100
scoresheets, 9, 165–159, 167–175
search engines, 29, 198–199
self-employment, 187–189
short-term work, 188–189
signing, bonus(es), 23, 116, 158, 174
Skadden, Arps, Slate, 99

skills, 3–6, 30, 36, 37, 149, 151, 167, 187
  accounting, 4, 83
  applicable, 192
  basic study, 103, 104
  becoming more specialized, 187
  clerical, 4
  creative, 97
  educational, 5
  from previous jobs, 4
  knowledge-based, 188
  marketable, 4
  physical, 4
  set of skills, 4
Snowy Day program, 99
Southwest Airlines, 34
St. Anthony Medical Center, 132
Stallard, Don, 193
standards, 17, 42, 44
  and values, 42
  ethical, 43, 129
  industry, 193
  importance to you, 54, 152, 168
  university, 105
Starbucks, 52, 118
stock options, 117
Summer Time Kids Camp, 84

## T

taking responsibility, 65
talents, creative, 5
taxes, 114, 188, 189
TDS Telecom, 48
Team Bank of America's Volunteer Network, 36
technology updates, 47
telecommuting, 20, 72, 73, 75, 76

# INDEX

temporary work, 191–193
  temp-to-hire, 191–193
temporary work, 192
tenure, 18, 58, 96, 116, 153, 169
  -based bonuses, 23
Texas Instruments, 84
theatre, community, 102
trade with other companies, 101
training, 5, 48, 104
  wellness, 95
transportation, 73, 102, 106
  issues, 86
  public, 20, 86, 155, 171
try different jobs, 192

## U

U.S. Census Bureau, 92
United Healthcare, 84
United Way, 131

## V

vacations, 94, 96, 187
  why we take, 184
value-added services, 102
valuing experience, 44
Vice President of People Development, 34
Vice President of People, 34
virtual office, 75
volunteering, 133
Volvo Heavy Truck, 126

## W

Walker Information, 43
websites, user-friendly,

Jobs Online, 197
Jobs.com, 197
Wells Fargo, 99
work/life balance, 19, 75, 76–77, 86
working styles, 9, 18–19, 42, 57–68
workplace,
   formality, 47, 60, 85
   politics, 19, 67, 68, 154
worksheets, 9, 10, 13, 144, 160–165, 180–185

## Y

Your Job Search, 12, 33, 35, 46, 48, 52, 61, 64, 72, 81, 94, 101, 104, 111, 118, 128, 132, 138, 148

# About the Authors

## Roger E. Herman

Roger E. Herman is Chief Executive Officer of The Herman Group, a management consulting, speaking, and training firm he founded in 1980. After serving as a Counterintelligence Special Agent during the Viet Nam era, he held a variety of management and sales positions in manufacturing, retail, distribution, and direct sales. He has also served as a City Manager. A graduate of Hiram College, Roger holds a master's degree from The Ohio State University in the field of Public Administration.

As a sought-after speaker, Roger earned the coveted Certified Speaking Professional (CSP) designation from the National Speakers Association. He is also a Certified Management Consultant (CMC)—one of only 15 people in the world to hold both the CSP and CMC. Roger is a member of the Society for Human Resource Management and the World Future Society.

A Strategic Business Futurist concentrating on workforce and workplace trends, Roger is consistently on target with his forecasts and his commentaries about trends are penetrating and provocative. Roger has published more than 600 articles, writes a column that is carried by a number of trade magazines, and frequently appears on radio and television talk shows.

He is Contributing Editor on workforce and workplace trends for *The Futurist* magazine. As the early advocate and author of *Keeping Good People* (first published in 1990), Roger is known as "the father of employee retention." He is widely recognized for his work in the field of workforce stability. The current edition of his seminal book is the No. 5 best-seller for the Society for Human Resource Management and has been featured by a number of book clubs.

## Joyce L. Gioia

Joyce L. Gioia is President of The Herman Group, based in Greensboro, North Carolina. A consultant since 1984, she is recognized as a Certified Management Consultant by the Institute of Management Consultants. A specialist in adding value, Joyce gained a national reputation for her work in direct marketing, product launches, and arranging strategic alliances. At the age of 28, she became the youngest magazine publisher in the country. Recognized as an innovator, she is known for her ability to understand and explain consumerism trends in the United States and in other countries and regions. She intertwines this knowledge with her work in the field of human resources to bring a totally new dimension to workforce stability strategy.

Joyce is a graduate of the University of Denver, and she holds a Masters of Business Administration from Fordham University. She also holds a Masters in Theology and a Masters in Counseling from The New Seminary in New York City. She has taught marketing at the university level at several schools.

A frequent speaker for corporate and trade association audiences, Joyce is a Professional Member of the World Future Society and the National Speakers Association. She is also a member of the American Society for Training and Development. A Fellow of the Workforce Stability Institute, Joyce is frequently cited in the news media for her expertise on workforce and workplace trends and internal marketing. She is regularly quoted in publications like *Business Week*, *Entrepreneur, Inc.*, and *The Christian Science Monitor*. She has also appeared on many radio and television talk shows and was featured by a cable network as well. Her concentration is communicating messages through organizational cultures to encourage people to remain productively with their employers for longer periods of times.

# ABOUT THE AUTHORS

Together, Joyce and Roger have co-authored three other books, including *Lean & Meaningful: A New Culture for Corporate America*, *Workforce Stability: Your Competitive Edge,* and *How to Become an Employer of Choice*. They balance the bottom line and the heart. The result is a clear business orientation with a strong human flavor.

## Andrew T. Perry

Andrew Perry is a writer, professor, and editor living in Greensboro, NC. He holds a degree in journalism from the University of Georgia and a Master of Fine Arts in Fiction from the University of North Carolina at Greensboro. He has worked in public relations in Atlanta and Boston, and currently splits his time between professional editing and writing, teaching writing and literature, and writing fiction. In free moments, he attends to the needs of a rather scruffy, half-wild pound dog named Maddie.

# Notes